10 ETERNAL TRUTHS

10 ETERNAL TRUTHS

Of Life, Healing, Death, Purpose,
and Creating All We Desire
in Our Lives

ERIK ALAN SWENSON

CONTENTS

DEDICATION

I dedicate this book to my
wife, my children,
my grandchildren,
and to all of humanity.

May one or more of the
truths we share bring ever
greater peace, joy, love,
light, health, and wellbeing
to you, and the manifestation
of ever more that you desire
in your life

PREFACE

Did you ever wonder if there is anything more to life, who we truly are, why some appear to experience all they desire, others far less, whether we can heal from whatever comes to exist within us, what truly happens when we die, or if we are somehow a part of something bigger than ourselves?

These questions arose within me throughout the earlier decades of my life, the answers presented themselves to me in ever varying ways throughout the those that followed.

As I progressively lived my life in ever greater harmony with these truths, the peace, joy, love, light, and wellbeing I experienced expanded ever further, as did the manifestation of all the more I desired to experience within my life.

The manners in which our lives unfold are not random.

As we become aware we are the creators of our lives, and how to do so consciously, the ability progressively expands within us to truly live our lives as we desire, and to create as we desire within our lives.

These truths similarly lead to having neither fear nor reservation relative to that which awaits us all when our life journeys become complete.

My purpose in writing this book is that even a single truth within it, if not the entirety of those identified, will bring greater peace, joy, love, and/or light to you, empower you to experience ever more of what you desire throughout the remainder of your life journey, and/or release any and all doubt, fear, or reservations relative to the eternal bliss that awaits us all as our life journeys become complete.

CHAPTER 1

Our Bodies

Our journey to presenting the truths we will identify within this book begins by establishing a foundation of awareness relative to the state of being of our human bodies.

The truth of our bodies begins with the expansion of our awareness relative to atoms.

As has been known for centuries, perhaps millennia, atoms are the building blocks of all that exist in physical form. Certainly, this includes all human beings as well.

While we tend to perceive atoms as physical, and, to a certain extent, this may be a truthful statement, Albert Einstein's focus on and understanding of physicality and energy combined with the advancement of technology that has taken place since combine to achieve a greatly expanded awareness of atoms, especially with regard to the truth of what exists within them.

The key awareness Einstein established relative to atoms is that their primary state of being is energy.

Prior understandings of atoms rested more greatly on the elements of physicality of the protons, neutrons, and electrons within them; Einstein's realization of their fundamental nature of energy leads to perceptions of atoms and the human body far beyond what most others had perceived historically.

Advancements in technology that have developed since his work further substantiate Einstein's realizations with clarity and precision.

As Einstein's awareness of atoms expanded, it became clear to him that the far greater, if not potentially absolute essence of atoms is the energy that exists within them.

An internet search today questioning what percent of each atom represents the physical characteristics within the atom will lead to credible scientific or research institutions similarly identifying that the totality of these physical components within each atom together constitute the tiniest fraction of 1% of each atom is actually physical matter.

The numbers of .00001% and .000001% have been common the past several years, some resources state there may be as many as twelve zeros preceding the number one, some quantum research reports there are literally no elements of physicality within atoms.

In the event it someday proven that tiniest aspects of physicality truly do exist within atoms, were there nothing more within each atom other than empty space, these elements would simply succumb to gravity and begin to formlessly fall, for there are no shells or other forms of substance surrounding atoms to hold them together.

Should the quantum perspective someday prove to truthful, no such mathematical calculation would be necessary, for the entirety of each atom would truly be empty space.

Whichever of these perspectives will someday be proven to be accurate matters not, for the truth relative to these building blocks of our bodies, and of all that exists in physical form, is that the vast entirety, if not totality of these individual aspects of life rests not in any elements of physicality that may exist within them, rather in the energy that exists within them, and empowers their existence.

This simple, absolute truth opens the door to a far greater understanding of the physicality of our human bodies.

As we have now established a clear understanding relative to the energetic nature of the building blocks that together construct the human body, it is accurate to begin referring to and perceiving the human body as a body of energy, or energy body, as the vast primary, if not entirety of the building blocks of which it exists consist of energy.

A second, related aspect that is important to identify to establish clarity as to the state of being, and the nature and functioning of the human body.

This second aspect is simple, yet perhaps equally as expansive as identifying energy as the primary state of being of the human body as energy.

If we return to an internet search asking the number of atoms that exist within the average human body, the answer is truly astounding; 7×10^{27}, or the number 7 followed by 27 zeros, 7,000,00 0,000,000,000,000,000,000,000.

This number is virtually inconceivable to comprehend relative to the sizes of human bodies; from a practical standpoint, this number is virtually infinite.

The third and final aspect we will define relative to atoms rests in the pondering of the orchestration of their individual lives and collective functioning within the human body, though this consideration applies equally to all atoms, regardless of the respective forms of life they have come forth to support.

Neither you nor I are in any way managing, orchestrating, or otherwise directing the individual or collective functioning of the 7,000,000,000,000,000,000,000,000,000 individual units of life within us in any given moment throughout our lives, let alone throughout the entirety of them.

Certainly there is a coordination, an orchestration taking place within every millisecond of the existence of our respective human energy bodies that allows our human bodies to exist, to function, for us to walk, talk, pick things up, hug someone, become lost in the radiance of sunrises or sunsets, hold our newborn babies in our arms, go to work, laugh, cry, experience endless joy, to the point of bliss, or deepest sorrows for whatever reasons within us.

Indeed, our bodies function in manners far beyond any that technology will ever be able to replicate, yet it is neither us nor our minds that create this masterful harmony within the virtually infinite individual elements of life within our bodies that allow us to have our life experiences as human beings.

Yet certainly there is an entity or source responsible for the functioning of our bodies, the intelligence and/or consciousness of which is formidable, if not limitless, for even the coordination of this many individual life units within one person is virtually inconceivable, let alone the coordinating of the functioning within the bodies of all the human beings who exist at any specific moment in time.

This same intelligence, or source, similarly enables, empowers, and coordinates the basic function of all life on earth, of the earth itself, and all else that exists upon it, of our solar system of our sun, and the planets and moons within it, not to mention the other solar systems, the galaxies within which they exist, the universes within which they exist, and the totality of all life and/or forms of physicality throughout all existence.

Regardless of who or what the source of such majestic orchestration may be, it is clear that it is being provided to all human beings throughout the entirety of our earthly journeys, and that it does so without regard to the manner in which we live our lives within our bodies.

And so, we are separate from this energy, source, or consciousness that brings the opportunity to live our lives to us; while, at the same time, this same energy, source, or consciousness equally exists within all other human beings, and within all that exists in physical form.

Who is the "we" that comes forth to live our life experience within our human body, and for whom our human bodies have come forth to provide this opportunity to us?

While we will expand upon this further, the "we" collectively, or each I individually, is a separate consciousness that comes forth to experience our human life experience.

We are not our bodies; instead, each of us is an individual consciousness, or soul, that has come forth to experience our human life experience in the energy body that has come forth to enable us to live our life experience.

We, the consciousness, or soul of who we are individually, are in partnership with our human energy bodies, so to speak, which have come forth to provide the opportunity for us to experience our life experience within our bodies.

The entirety of the characteristics we have defined together form the foundation for Eternal Truth Number One:

Our bodies are vessels of energy that have come forth to enable us, our consciousness, or souls, the eternal aspects of who we are, to live our current life experience.

CHAPTER 2

The Energy Within

As we shift our focus to expanding our awareness relative to the energy within our bodies, it is optimal to initially consider the roles it plays within our bodies.

This energy enables and empowers the existence of the virtually infinite numbers of atoms within our bodies, the seamless coordination of groupings of these atoms into the molecules within our bodies, the seamless coordination of groupings of these molecules into the cells within our bodies, and the interdependent functioning of each of these forms together to enable the functioning of the entirety of our respective human energy bodies.

It also continually performs these functions throughout the entirety of our lives without any conscious awareness, guidance, or participation by us in any way.

It is certainly truthful to begin by defining this energy as intelligent, for the cumulative awareness and coordination necessary to coordinate each of these varying individual elements of existence, as well as in their collective forms of molecules and cells within each of our energy bodies is, at a minimum, formidable.

As we further contemplate the vastness of the intelligence of this energy as it simultaneously empowers and enables these very same individual building blocks of units of life of atoms and collective groupings of molecules and cells within all other human beings, and also within every single plant, animal, mountain, stream, ocean, and every other form of physical existence on earth, as well as the earth itself, it is certainly reasonable to begin to perceive such intelligence as profound.

Expanding our awareness of the vastness of this same energy fulfilling these same roles relative to the sun, the fellow planets, moons, and varying forms of life within our solar system, it is further clear that the intelligence coordinating the existence and internal functioning of each and every form of physical existence within our solar system, as well as the perfect harmony and coordination of the movement and interactions of the elements of physicality within it, is progressively more inconceivable to the human mind.

As science and ever advancing technologies are making us aware the vast expanse of our solar system is but a minute fraction of the totality of the elements of physicality within our galaxy, which similarly represent a minute fraction of the totality of the elements within our universe, which similarly represent a minute fraction of the totality of the elements within all other universes beyond ours, all of which are similarly held in as perfect harmony with one another, it becomes crystal clear that a far more accurate descriptive of the energy that empowers and enables the existence of all that exists in physical form is the term infinite intelligence.

Were the essence, or source of this energy, intentionally controlling every single action each and every individual single element of physicality within all physical existence, it would, in the process, be eternally limiting the range of experiences each and every aspect of itself experiences, as well as the experiences and consciousness of itself throughout eternity.

However, as each and every human being has the ability to stand or sit, turn left or right, jump up in the air or into the water, to be happy or sad, to love or hate, to choose to be a janitor or a rocket scientist, or truly live their lives in whatever ways they desire, it is clear that all human beings, as well as all of the virtually limitless other individual aspects of this infinite intelligence, have the ability to live their lives in manners that are similarly unique within their respective life forms.

This is the purpose for which physicality came forth; for the oneness within which all exists to eternally expand through the entirety of the experiences all of the individual aspects of itself experience throughout eternity, with no limitations.

The vastness of this truth, of this awareness, of this divinity within all physicality, could also be defined as consciousness.

This consciousness has existed within all that has ever been in physical form, it exists within all that exists in physical form today and will exist within all that will ever come to be in physical form because it is the primary, if not sole aspect within each and every unit of life of all atoms, the building blocks of all that exist in physical form.

This true nature of this source of infinite intelligence becomes clear as we reflect upon its eternal presence within all that exists in physical form, and its choice to allow all the individual aspects of itself to live their lives in whatever manners they choose throughout the entirety of each physical life experience they choose to experience.

The true, innate, eternal nature of this consciousness, this spirit, this source of all life, is unconditional love.

This source of all life loves and treasures each and every aspect of itself that ever come to be in physical form that it continually enables and empowers the existence of all life throughout the entirety of its physical experience and allow each individual aspects of itself to experience their existence in whatever ways they desire throughout the entirety of their physical life experience.

It is important to define and clarify the term unconditional love.

It is the loving, cherishing, and treasuring of all that is, throughout the entirety of the existence of all individual aspects of itself, throughout eternity, while enabling and empowering all to live as each desire throughout eternity.

Certainly, there is a source of this energy, for were there no source, no such energy would exist, and it would be as logical and accurate to refer to this source of all life as creator, for it is the presence of the energy of this eternal consciousness that enables and empowers all physical life to come to be.

In simplicity, we have now defined the creator as the source of all life, all that comes to be in physical form as what has been created, and the energy, or spirit that exists within all that has been created.

This energy, this spirit, is what has historically been taught of, or passed down as the holy spirit.

While the intent of this book is not to focus on any specific religion or faith practice, the existence of these three aspects of the divine correlate directly with biblical references relative to the Father, Son, and Holy Spirit.

The creator is the source of all life (the Father), the created represents all life that comes into existence (the Son), and the spirit that enables and empowers all that exists in physical form to exist is the spirit of the creator (the Holy Spirit).

The clarity we are achieving relative to the essence of the spirit of the creator being within us, and all that exists, has wonderful repercussions relative to the truth of who we are.

As the vast primary, if not sole aspect of our bodies is the spirit of the within them, it is accurate to state that none are ever separate from the divine, for all are individual aspects of the divine.

As the divine is of infinite value and worth, so too are each of us of infinite value and worth, exactly as we are, for each of us are eternally unique expressions, or extensions, of the divine.

As the spirit of the divine empowers and enables all life to be, and this spirit exists within us too, the ability to create exists within us too. We will expand upon this further in the following chapter.

The characteristics and aspects we have defined relative to the energy within the human body forms the foundation for Eternal Truth Number Two:

> *The energy within us, that empowers and enables our existence, is the divine spirit of unconditional love of the creator.*

CHAPTER 3

We Are Creators,
How We Create

As the essence of all that exists in physical form is the energy, the spirit that enables and empowers all human beings and all other forms of physicality to exist, it would certainly be possible for this same source of life within which all exist to somehow control, limit, or otherwise direct the range or scope of experiences for all the individual aspects of itself that come to be.

And yet how contrary that would be to the eternal growth, expansion, and evolution of the oneness within which all exists, as well as each of the virtually limitless individual aspects of itself.

The creator lacks nothing, and all that has ever been, all that exists today, and all that will ever come to be throughout eternity exists within it.

Imagine being the consciousness of the totality of all that is.

While it could possibly bring joy for a period of existence to bask in a state of gratitude and awareness of the fullness and entirety that you are in nonphysical, aka formlessness, certainly it is likely that a being of such consciousness wound benefit from, deeply appreciate, and thrive ever more exceptionally through ever more opportunities to experience itself in ever new ways throughout eternity.

This eternal consciousness brought physical existence into being to allow virtually limitless, ever expanding individual aspects, or extensions of itself, to experience ever new life experiences in ever new forms and ways throughout eternity.

Would such consciousness choose to limit the life experiences of the extensions of itself in any way, the experiences of itself would be limited as well.

Instead, the source of all life naturally experiences eternal growth and expansion through the entirety of experiences it and each and every individual expression of itself choose to experience throughout eternity, just as all such individual aspects of itself similarly expand through each such life experience it chooses throughout eternity.

The "reciprocity of oneness", so to speak, in which the creator exists within all that is, and all that is exists within the oneness of the creator, assures endless eternal growth and expansion for individual extensions of the creator and the oneness of the creator within which all exists.

It is for this reason the energy, or spirit of the oneness within which all exists eternally exists within each and every individual aspect of itself that comes to be throughout eternity.

The source that creates worlds, solar systems, galaxies, universes, and all the life forms that exist within each of these eternally exists within all that has ever been, all that exists today, and all that will ever come into being.

This presence of this spirit of the creator within all that exists in physicality innately results in each and every individual aspect of itself influencing their respective life experience based upon the manner in which they focus the energy within them.

While the manners and opportunities in which the seemingly endless varieties of variations of life are inherently able to influence their lives depend on the form of the respective physical vessels they choose for their life journeys, the range of manners and opportunities in which human beings can influence their lives is virtually limitless.

From the food we eat to the action steps we do or don't take, the activities we choose to engage in or avoid, the employment or hobbies er choose, the endlessly differing relationships we are able to experience with ourselves and with others, the manners in which we interact with other forms of physicality, such as the animals or nature around us, or bright, shiny things we desire, whether we choose to be joyful, loving, peaceful, or disappointed, angry, or vengeful, it is truly up to every single human being to live their life as they desire.

As physical existence was created to allow all the individual aspects of the oneness that choose to live physical life experience to experience their respective life journeys in whatever ways they desire, physicality was masterfully created in a manner in which all forms of life that come to be in physical form innately communicate into the universe of physicality, so to speak.

In turn, the innate consciousness within the entirety of physicality (which we will refer to as "the universe" going forward) is fundamentally programmed to bring ever more to each such individual expression of the creator in physical form that is in alignment with the communications they emit into it.

As energy, or the spirit of the creator, is the common element of all forms of physical life, it is similarly the manner through which all forms of physical existence communicate into the universe.

In essence and simplicity, as all forms of physicality consist primarily, if not solely, of energy, and as energy naturally vibrates, it is the vibrations each and every form of life in physical existence innately emit that the universe perceives.

As the essence of the source of all life is unconditional love, physicality was created in a manner in which the universe perceives the vibrations each and every form of physicality emit into it, which engages the universe to bring ever more to such life forms that is in alignment with the vibrations they emit into it.

The vibrations that every single individual aspect of the creator emit, including those of human beings, represent the universal form of linguistics in which all forms of physical life communicate into the universe.

The innate programming of the universe to being ever more that is in alignment with the vibrations all extensions of the creator who come to exist emit into it naturally leads to eternal growth and expansion of all such aspects, as well as the oneness within which all exist.

The virtually limitless abilities for human beings to create rest in the awareness they are naturally creating throughout the entirety of their waking states within their lives, regardless of whether they are aware they are doing so, aka creating consciously, or not aware they are doing so, aka creating unconsciously.

The general lack of awareness of these basic, fundamental principles of physical existence throughout the evolution of humanity has resulted in relatively large percentages of people unintentionally creating their lives in manners that have not been in alignment with their desires.

To the contrary, many have created, and/or are continuing to create today, in manners that are opposed to their desires.

Unfulfillment of desires is never the result of the universe's inability to manifest what each desire, nor is it due to the universe in any way filtering or otherwise influencing the desires people may communicate into it.

Instead, unfulfilled desires, or creations or experiences in contrast to our desires, are the result of people not realizing they are constantly creating throughout the entirety of their lifetimes or knowing how to create in alignment with their desires.

This lack of awareness naturally leads to unintentional communications with the universe in manners that are not in alignment with their desires.

While the awareness of this absolute, eternal truth relative to all physical existence has been known, spoken of, taught of, and even lived by varying individuals and/or groupings of people for millennia, this truth is not common knowledge of most of humanity as of the creation of this book.

Examples of those who have achieved this awareness include:

- Albert Einstein: "Everything is energy and that's all there is to it. Match the frequency of the reality you want and you cannot help but get that reality."
- Buddha: "We are shaped by our thoughts; we become what we think;"
- Jesus: "Ask, and it will be given to you; seek, and you will find; knock, and the door will be opened to you.", and "All things are possible for those who believe."

Each of these individuals were correct in their statements as to how we create.

In simplicity, as we define something we choose to experience in our lives for even the briefest of moments, we are, in essence, planting an energetic seed into the universe for us to experience whatever it is we have defined within our lives.

Once planted, would we leave such seeds to be, so to speak, especially depending on the feelings and/or vibrations we emitted as we focused on our new desire, it would naturally come to be in perfect time if we did not in any way offer vibrations in contrast to our new desire coming to be in our lives.

And yet, once a desire has come to be, we often focus on it again, perhaps even often, and the vibrations we exist as we do so sill directly influence our ability to experience the manifestation of our desire within our lives.

Should our progressive focus on our desire be the positive, joyful feeling of having whatever it is we desire in our lives, we will be assisting the vibrational seed we desire in coming to be.

Should it instead be of worry it will not come to be, our minds telling us we don't have the resources for it to come to be, or that we are not worthy of having it, we will be thwarting the vibrational seed we desire in coming to be.

Einstein was 100% correct in identifying these truths, for the frequency we are emitting when we sense or feel the presence of our desire in our life is the frequency the universe perceives, begins to focus on, and match back to us in our lives in ever expanding ways.

The perspectives of Buddha and Jesus are equally correct relative to the creation process, as well as key indicators of how people unintentionally create in contrast to their desires.

Buddha's comment similarly identifies one potential action that can unintentionally keep what we desire from us.

Once we define a desire, should we allow the focus of our mind to shift to not deserving our desire, not having the financial resources to achieve our desire, or doubts that our desire will come to be, such perspectives naturally influence the outcome we experience by keeping such desires from us.

This is because the universe is fulfilling the conflicting, if not stronger and/or more consistent vibrations in alignment with not receiving what we desire.

Jesus' comments are equally true, for all we ask for, and/or otherwise seek to experience will naturally come to be as we communicate our desires to into the universe and believe they will come to be.

As the universe's eternal, fundamental programming is to bring ever more to us that is in energetic alignment with that which we emit into it, the vibrations of our continuing thoughts relative to our desires either keep what we desire from us or result in manifesting the opposite of what we desire.

As an example, in the event a person seeks a beautiful relationship with a life partner, yet cannot release the fear, concern, and/or worry their mind presents to them due to harm they experienced in one or more past relationships, any new person they engage in a relationship with until they achieve greater vibrational alignment with their desire will likely, if not assuredly be in alignment with those they no longer desire.

While this is likely the last thing the person would ever want to experience again, the emitting of such contrary vibrations would literally keep those capable of having the relationship that is truly desired away from them or cause such relationship with one they could likely experience what they desire with to fail.

Jesus' latter quote represents the fundamental essence of consciously creating what we desire in our lives.

Countless times throughout my life I listened to teachings, read, or heard sermons based upon bible passages which referenced Jesus assisting people in experiencing healing.

From my earliest years on I remember perceiving the love with which he did so, while also the statement "Your faith has made you well." he shared with those he assisted in healing.

Would one simply plant the seed of their desire, and believe it would be so, with no qualms, reservations, doubt, or "mind chatter", aka comments or perspectives our minds share with us in contrast to it, the universe will begin paving pathways to bring our desires to us.

Jesus' initial quote is equally truthful relative to the creation process, for as we continue to ask, seek, and find what we desire, each of these represent vibrations in alignment with our desires coming to be.

Yes, we are the creators of our lives, whether we are doing so consciously or unconsciously.

We similarly grow and expand regardless of which of these manners in which we create, for the outcomes of either such form of creation, whether they are in alignment with or in contrast to our desire, lead us to experience our lives from new perspectives and/or circumstances, which naturally lead to new desires arising within us.

Were we simply living one life experience, one could perceive our manifestations to be of success or failure, depending on the outcome of our creations.

As eternal beings who choose ever new life experiences throughout eternity, there is no losing or failure so to speak, only eternal winning, so to speak, as all that we experience cause us to define new desires, which naturally leads to our continued growth and expansion throughout eternity.

Thus said, we are eternally welcome to create in alignment with our desires, and should we choose to do so, the joy and love and light we experience within such lives is as limitless and ever expanding as our ability to create within our lives.

The entirety of the above discussion forms the foundation for Eternal Truth Number Three:

We are the creators of our lives, we create through the vibrations we emit into the universe, which naturally engage the universe to draw ever more to us that is in alignment with the vibrations we emit throughout the entirety of our life journey.

CHAPTER 4

Aligning With Our Desires

In our awareness that we create in our lives through the vibrations we emit into the universe, the intent of this chapter is to expand our understanding relative to the primary manners in which we create and explore specific perspectives and/or practices capable of assisting us in emitting vibrations in ever greater alignment with our desires.

Our thoughts, words, beliefs, and action steps represent the primary sources of the vibrations we emit in our lives.

Our thoughts represent vibrations through the feelings and/or emotions we emit while focusing on and/or experiencing them.

A quick thought can be easily received and fulfilled, such as the sensing of our hunger, and finding a place – possibly the perfect place in that moment – to find food we desire in little to no time.

While large percentages of the thoughts we think are generally noncreative, as they do not occur often, or have minimal feelings, emotions, or vibration associated with them, common underlying patterns of such thoughts are progressively ever more creative in our lives.

As an example, one who chooses to view their life and/or the world around them with feelings of appreciation most every day is creating a life pathway in which they will naturally experience ever more that brings feelings and/or emotions of appreciation to them.

Alternatively, one who chooses to view their life and/or the world around them with feelings of lack, judgment, criticizing others, or consistently complains about things or other individuals or groupings of people is creating a life pathway in which they will naturally experience ever more that brings such feelings and/or emotions to them.

It is also helpful to understand that even a single thought we focus on briefly has the ability to come into being, especially if accompanied by strong emotions, such as incredible joy or love, or rage or anger.

Our thoughts are powerful sources of the vibrations we emit into the universe.

The vibrations resulting from the beliefs we hold within us are similarly creative.

Beliefs of value or worth are primary in life, in that those who believe they are of value and/or worth naturally emit vibrations of empowerment and positivity, which draws ever more experiences with people, events, and experiences to them that are in alignment with the perspectives of value, worth, and positivity they hold within them.

Alternatively, those who do not believe they are of value or worth naturally emit vibrations of lack of value or worth, powerlessness, doubt, and/or negativity, which draws ever more experiences with people, events, and experiences to them that are in alignment with these perspectives they hold within them.

This truth relative to the influence of our beliefs similarly applies relative to perspectives of what we can or are not able to accomplish.

The creative power, or energy, of the universe exists within us; as it is there for us to focus with, aka direct as we desire; the only limitations to what we can create rest in those we perceive within us, and, therefore, emit into the universe.

A perfect example of this lies in the awareness humanity previously held that it was not possible for a human being to run a 4-minute mile.

A man by the name of Roger Bannister developed a belief within him that it could be done, he did so in 1954; and many others have done so since that time.

His steadfast holding to the belief he could do so, accompanied by the action steps he took to prepare himself to do so, together resulted in the outcome he desired, and knew he could achieve.

Others who followed were able to do so because his achievement of this feat opened their awareness to the possibility they could accomplish this same feat as well.

The third primary source of the vibrations we emit into the universe is the words that we speak.

Words we speak to ourselves silently are creative; those we voice to ourselves or others can be even more so due the strengthened vibrational emission they represent due to the engagement of the elements of physicality within our energy bodies as they are being expressed.

The words I am, or I am not, or I can, or I cannot, are powerfully creative, for through them we are speaking to the universe as to who we are, and what we are or are not capable of.

Whether spoken once or consistently more so over time, whatever words follow these creative statements are defining who we are to the universe through the clear, directive vibrations that accompany them.

Due to the powerful nature of words relative to the creation process, those who seek to create consciously will benefit from developing an awareness as to whether the words flowing through them as they speak are in harmony with our desires, or in contrast to them.

Plain and simple, if they feel good, kind, caring, loving, positive, supportive, or of having our desire in our lives, they are in alignment with our desires.

Should they feel the opposite of these, or should we experience any fear, doubt, worry, or concern while speaking them, it is best to literally stop ourselves from time to time, including mid-sentence, if necessary, when they don't feel good, rather than continuing to express the contrast they represent to any, if not all of our desires coming to be.

The additional primary influence on the vibrations we emit into the universe rests in the action steps we take in our lives.

As the action steps we take are in manners our minds perceive to be appropriate for us based upon the underlying thoughts and beliefs we hold within us, similar to the words that we speak, the physical enactment of them represent powerful influences on what we create in our lives.

We take action steps in our lives that based upon the combination of thoughts, beliefs, and abilities we perceive within us.

One whose thoughts and beliefs relative to who they are include being of value, worth, and capable will take action steps in alignment with these. As the universe draws ever more people, events, and experiences to us in alignment with the vibrations we emit into it, such underlying feelings will support the action steps such individuals choose, and lead to the outcome they desire which led them to take such action steps.

Alternatively, one who internally perceives themselves as of little or no value and/or their abilities to be lacking will generally limit the action steps they take in their lives and tend to feel fear should they consider action steps their mind perceives to be beyond their worth or abilities to experience.

As an example, perhaps such an individual meets or befriends someone they feel attracted to, and would like to explore a relationship with, thinks so little of themselves that their mind tells them they are not worthy, or that person could never be interested in them, and so they never take the action step of asking the person out on a date, or expressing their interest in such a relationship with them.

One who perceives themselves to be of value and worth will likely take the step, perhaps at what they perceive to be a strategic moment, to tell the other how they feel, which opens the door for them to experience the relationship they desire with the other person.

While the source of each of these differing perspectives are those our mind presents to us, clearly the outcome of the first results in taking action steps in alignment with our desires, whereas the latter results in not taking action steps that are in alignment with our desires.

Whether the thoughts or beliefs we hold within us, the words we speak to ourselves or others, or the action steps we take, those who choose to become ever more adept at consciously creating in their lives will be well served by practices and/or perspectives that assist them in shifting the vibrations they emit to be in ever greater alignment with their desires.

Such processes to do so need not be difficult or invasive, rather simply a progressive lessening of emitting vibrations that keep our desires from us, while progressively increasing of emitting vibrations that allow our desires to come to be.

As the reasons we want all that desire are to bring and/or experience ever greater peace, joy, love, and/or light in our lives, the choice to periodically focus on anything or anyone who elicits such feelings or emotions within us will similarly bring ever more of our desires to us.

Calling or visiting a friend or other loved one that brings joy and happiness to us each day is a simple, yet wonderful way to assist us in shifting the vibrations we emit.

Taking a walk on the sunniest days; or in a raincoat on the rainiest of days cherishing the nourishing the rain is providing can be a joyful and fun filled experience as well.

Gazing up at the moon or stars that fill the skies at night, at the flowers around us during the day, at children playing at the playground, riding our bike in an area we especially enjoy, holding hands with a partner, child, or grandchild, sitting quietly focusing on our breath, perhaps accompanied by a statement we tell ourselves such as "I am so grateful for the life I am living.", or "I feel so incredibly blessed in my life" are all stepping stones that are capable of assisting us in emitting vibrations in alignment with our desires.

Witnessing the beauty, perfection, and majesty of the flow of water in a brook stream, or river, the waves of a lake or ocean, the stillness and majesty of a forest of trees, hills or mountains, even of the forms of life around us daily, such as the birds, butterflies, frogs or toads or squirrels, blades of grass, or dandelions, the appreciation of any and all forms of nature and/or of life all similarly assist us in emitting vibrations in alignment with our desires.

Even sharing a simple statement of gratitude, or good morning or good afternoon greeting with another, represents the emitting of vibrations of care and wellbeing that are in alignment with our desires, with our higher selves, with the creator, and with the universe, which will bring ever more such in alignment with such experiences into our lives.

Absent any of the above practices, even the choice to feel good, loving, caring, joyful, and appreciative of ourselves, others, or whatever we choose to focus on will assist our desires in coming to be.

The universe only knows "yes" as it seeks to expand all that individual extensions of the divine emit into it.

Humanity has the ability to speak in yeses and no's, and while the meanings of the differentiation between them are understandable within human minds, no such form of interpretation or filtering takes place within the universe.

The universe simply – and absolutely – brings ever more people, events, and experiences to people in alignment with the energetic essence of what they choose to focus on.

And so, the opportunity exists within us throughout the entirety of our earthly journey to choose to emit vibrations in alignment with our desires, with our souls, and with the creator, as frequently and/or consistently as possible.

There are two additional perspectives that will be helpful for us to address for those who seek to consciously create in their lives.

The first is that, while we are always creating throughout the entirety of the awake (non-sleep) state in our lives, as the average human mind thinks approximately 6,000 thoughts per day, we are not creating 6,000 different things in a day.

Instead, we are creating ever more progressively based upon the combination of the intensity of our desires, aka the vibrations we emit into the universe relative to them, the frequency, aka continuity of the thoughts we are consistently emitting into the universe, and whether we truly believe they will come to be in our lives.

A strong desire focused on for even a minute or two can lead to the manifestation of such desire in our lives if it is accompanied by the belief it could come to be.

A less strong, perhaps even subtle vibration that is more frequently focused upon, or present within us can lead to the manifestation of what we desire in our lives, absent accompanying doubts that it could come to be.

Alternatively, regardless of which of these manners our desires arose within us, and, therefore, were communicated into the universe via the vibrations we emit relative to them, the presence of fairly frequent to continual doubt relative to such desires arising within us can be sufficient to keep the manifestation of such desires in our lives from us.

Becoming adept at releasing perspectives that do not feel in alignment within us and shifting our focus to anything that brings positive feelings or emotions to us represents a progressively more simple, effective way to create all the more we desire in our lives.

Even the insertion of no thought as we perceive perspectives that do not feel in alignment within us, such as focusing on our breathing, or marveling at anything or anyone we see around us, or the music playing or absolute quiet in that moment naturally help to shift our vibrations in manners which lessen or eliminate the emitting of vibrations that are not in alignment with our desires.

As the creation process is all about vibrations, while such practices may appear to be questionable to our minds, they directly influence the vibrations we emit, which directly influence whether our desires come to be in our lives.

The second additional perspective to assist those who seek to consciously create in their lives is that, unlike traveling to a specific destination and remaining there forever, the process of aligning with our desires is not a single destination forever remain within once we arrive there, nor would we want it to be a single destination for us.

Instead, in any given moment we may be in alignment with some or all the desires we seek to create in our lives; at times we may not be in alignment with or may even be in direct contrast to some or all the desires that we seek to create in our lives.

It is truly not possible to be in alignment with all our desires every moment of our lives, nor did we come forth with the intent to do so, as contrast is among the greatest source from which new desires arise within us, and, depending on such contrast we are experiencing, we may be in our out of alignment while experiencing it.

Contrast and the new desires that arise from it are inherent aspects of our human journeys.

We came forth to sift and sort, to choose ever new desires, and emitting ever new vibrations due to the desires that have arisen from the contrast we've experienced is the primary key to living our life filled with the peace, joy, love, light, and the creation of all the more we desire.

While we can't live our lives wrong, so to speak, for the living of our lives is always in perfect alignment with the eternal, everlasting, ever expanding consciousness of who we are, living our lives in ever greater alignment with our desires will assist us in experiencing all the more of our desires within our current lifetimes.

The totality of these perspectives combine to lead us to define Eternal Truth Number Four:

> *The ability to live our live in ever greater alignment with our desires awaits us in every moment of our lives: those who choose to do so will naturally attract ever more of what they desire into their lives throughout the remainder of their life journey.*

CHAPTER 5
The Ability to Heal

The truths we have defined relative to human beings continually creating throughout the entirety of their lives and that we create based upon what we focus on ideally position us to address the topic of healing our physical energy bodies.

Among the most common, and, at times concerning challenges people face is the ability for them to heal from whatever health imbalances have come to exist within their energy bodies.

Fortunately, as the energy, or spirit of the creator that exists within us is eternally programmed to bring to us ever more to us in alignment with that which we emit into it, there are no limits to what we can achieve.

As the awareness of progressively ever more people expands to include the ability to engage this spirit, to assist us in healing from whatever health imbalance has come to exist within our energy bodies, the health and wellbeing of many individually, as well as the entirety of humanity, will progressively differ ever more greatly from the proliferation of health imbalances that exist as of the writing of this book.

This is not because this book somehow makes people more worthy of healing than they were before, for each is worthy of receiving all they desire, throughout eternity, including the healing of whatever health imbalances have come to exist within their existing human energy bodies.

Instead, it is because ever more are becoming aware of the ability to heal that innately exists within them, whether through this book or other sources, and choosing to consciously engage the spirit of the creator within all to achieve the healing of whatever health imbalances have come to exist within their energy bodies.

Whatever has come to be, has come to be to this point in our lives, yet whatever comes to be from this point forward for those who choose to live in ever greater vibrational alignment with their desires will be in ever greater alignment with their desires, including the restoration of health and wellbeing to their human energy bodies.

And so, we will now identify and explore perspectives to assist those who desire in creating a healing journey in their lives.

Imagine a person you care for or love experiencing a health imbalance.

Having discussed the creation process in great detail, it is likely clear the creation of the wellbeing they now desire rests in a shift of their vibration to that of joy, peace, happiness, love, and wellbeing.

Further applying our awareness of the creation process to our ability to heal, we realize that the more one focuses on whatever health imbalance has come to exist within their energy body, the greater such imbalance, and perhaps others in energetic alignment with it, will expand in their lives due to the continuing vibrations they are emitting focused on such imbalance within their energy body.

Our awareness of the creation process also leads us to an understanding that emotions of worry or fear relative to any topics, including that of health imbalances that have come to exist within our energy bodies, result in us emitting further expanded vibrations into the universe in alignment with the experience we no longer seek to experience, rather than the outcome of health and wellbeing that we truly desire.

These base awareness's combine to lead us to the key focus of the first conscious healing process we will identify being that of replacing the perspectives of worry, fear, or of the imbalance with perspectives that result in us experiencing feelings and emotions of peace, joy, love, light, and the health and wellbeing of our human energy bodies.

The greater and more consistently we experience each of these in our lives, regardless of the specific focuses we are choosing to lead us to experience such feelings and emotions, the greater and more consistently we naturally draw to us in alignment with these vibrations, including the health and wellbeing of our human energy bodies.

As simple as this healing process can be for us, among the greatest challenges it represents is our ability to maintain far greater energetic alignment with the outcome of healing we desire throughout our healing process, rather than the imbalance that has come to be.

Living in a vacuum, so to speak, would likely be an easy environment to achieve such balance in, as it would be up to the individual alone to create and maintain this state of healing and wellbeing vibrations within them; yet all innately live their lives amidst varying forms and degrees of contrast.

Such forms or degrees of contrast when health imbalances arise often include the health care providers they choose, many of whom are unaware of the clear correlation of the manners in which we focus and the outcome of healing we desire.

Further, significant percentages of well-intended medical practices throughout the world that are rooted in a continued focus on the imbalance also including communicating statistics and, at times, even perilous outcomes others who were similarly unaware of the creation process previously experienced.

From a creation standpoint, such communications and practices are unintentionally in greater alignment with the continued existence and/or expansion of the health imbalance than with the intended healing of it.

It is also common within many such practices to introduce a fight mentality in which it is perceived the individual is fighting against the imbalance that has come to be.

As the fundamental nature of fighting anything rests in a continued focus on that which they are fighting against until it has been "conquered", or no longer exist within them, such continued focus, combined with the naturally heightened emotions inherent in fighting against anything, is in far greater alignment with the perpetuation and/or expansion of what is no longer desired, rather than that of the healing and wellbeing that is truly desired.

The natural outcomes of such fear or anger-based perspectives for those unaware of their ability to heal include feelings and/or emotions of ever greater worry and/or fear within them, which similarly contribute to the expansion of the imbalance they are experiencing, and/or draw other experiences in energetic alignment with the imbalance to them.

Based upon the clarity we have defined relative to the creation process, those who seek to consciously create healing in their lives – or virtually anything else in their lives – will be best served to not in any way attempt to "push against' or fight whatever it is they no longer choose to experience, rather to ever more progressively shift their vibrations to those of alignment with peace, joy, love, light, and the presence of the wellbeing - or whatever else it is they desire – already being in their life.

As consistent periodic focus on a topic represents among the greatest contributors to the vibrations we emit relative to such topics, it is especially helpful for those who seek to create healing in their lives to achieve and develop practices and manners to maintain vibrations in alignment with these vibrations ever more consistently throughout their healing journey.

The more practiced we become at consciously creating, the progressively easier it becomes for us to sift and sort through the contrast we experience, and to shift our vibrations by becoming as emotionally engaged as possible with all that feels in alignment within us, and as emotionally disengaged as possible with all that does not feel in alignment within us.

Becoming ever more adept at releasing insights or perspectives we experience in our healing journeys that do not feel in alignment with us, such as statistics that could otherwise bring fear to us if we were not aware of the ability to heal within us, and focusing all the more greatly on those that do, such as peace, joy, love, light, happiness, or our wellbeing, is perhaps the most helpful, key, primary choice we can make to lead us to the outcome of health and wellbeing we desire through this healing process.

A simple statement such as "I feel so blessed to have such wonderful people assisting me in my healing journey." is a powerful tool those who are consciously creating their healing may wish to keep in their awareness and repeat to themselves when any who are involved in their healing journey present any forms of perspectives, language, or prognosis to them that do not feel to be in alignment with the healing they desire.

Perhaps even repeating such a statement to ourselves two or three times, saying it and quietly out loud as those who shared such perspectives walk away, or sharing the comment with a close friend or family member who similarly understands the creation process who is with you at such times, immediately shifts the energy of such statement or perspectives shared into that which is in alignment with the healing journey they are creating.

There is an additional, sensitive aspect that is important to discuss relative to our ability to heal through this process in our lives; this aspect is the potential power of prayer, and the manner in which we pray.

It is common for many who experience health imbalances to pray.

As all that we do represents the emitting of vibrations into the universe, all the more so when accompanied by heightened feelings and/or emotions when focused on our health imbalance, or in such communications with the creator, it is optimal for those who choose to experience healing in their lives to pray in a manner that reflects our appreciation for the outcome of health and wellbeing we desire, rather than the health imbalance, or fear or worry of which such imbalance could lead to.

Even prayers of appreciation of anything, anyone, any of the experiences we have already had in our lives, or of the experiences we choose to create going forward in our lives are all communications the creator immediately perceives, and through which the vibrations we emit while expressing them are perceived by universe, which the universe immediately begins to respond to by drawing ever more to us in alignment with such vibrations of appreciation.

As a key, fundamental goal of this healing process rests in shifting our vibration to that of health, happiness, and wellbeing, virtually any thought, perception, or feeling of joy, happiness, or wellbeing will assist us in experiencing ever more in alignment with each of these in our lives.

The following activities or practices are being shared to provide some ideas that could feel in alignment for those who choose to heal through this process to assist them in maintaining a vibration in alignment with the health and wellbeing you desire throughout their respective healing journey.

In no specific order, these practices and activities include:

1. Focus on something you appreciate for 1 – 2 minutes or more each morning when you awake, and each night when you go to bed; perhaps even once or twice or more times a day if you would like. Whether a sunrise or sunset, a thought of someone you love, a memory that brings happiness or joy to you, the radiance of each person assisting you in your healing journey, or reflecting on some of the most beautiful or otherwise meaningful moments in your life, the more you do so, the more consistent your vibration of peace, love, joy, happiness, and wellbeing is being communicated into and received by the universe.

2. Perhaps consider this same practice after any conversations or occurrences that do not feel in alignment with your desire. Consider taking a deep breath or two following such situations, and tell yourself "How perfect it is that their perspective relative to whatever has taken place is as right

for them as my perspective is right for me", or a phrase such as "How grateful I am for the assistance this person is providing in my healing journey" should such interaction have taken place with someone assisting you in your healing journey.

3. Send a note of care or appreciation to someone you love, or to thank someone who touched you in a meaningful way in your life.

4. Call someone to tell them you love them, and if they ask about your health, tell them you're doing great, and feeling and getting better each and every new day.

5. Find a loved one or a friend who is open to understanding the perspectives you are following to restore balance to your energy body, and is "all in" to the idea of having fun conversations with you, doing fun things with you, laughing with you, loving you, who will listen if you need to share something personal or otherwise important to you, while only briefly if you're temporarily out of alignment, and remind you that you've got this, you are rock starring this, and you know darn well you'll still be having fun together 20 or 30 or 40 or more years from now.

6. Envision a faraway birthday such as age 90, imagine yourself in a setting with your family, perhaps even children, grandchildren, or even great grandchildren, the candles surrounding the number 90 on the cake are lit, you look around at all the balloons, and everyone having so much fun, and blow the candles out. Feel the richness and awesomeness of this experience, the pride, the joy, the love for a minute or two... perhaps even bask in it for a bit longer... for in the process you are planting a powerful seed for it to be.

7. Expand upon this same example by envisioning your dentures falling out as you were blowing the candles out, and you and everyone else in the room exploding with laughter. Laughter is among the most powerful of emotions, the more we experience, the more and stronger vibrations we emit that are most certainly in alignment with our health, wellbeing, and longevity.

8. Watch funny movies, watch movies that make you feel empowered, that have happy endings, that are joyful, or loving. Watch as many of them as you can, daily, if not more often, as the feelings you experience and the amount of time you experience them lead to vibrations in alignment with the healing and wellbeing you desire.

9. In the event you are aware of a nagging or hurtful memory that has somehow come to exist within you, allow it to come into your awareness and tell yourself "I know that I did the best I could do in this situation.", "I know this experience has contributed to me being the person I am today", and/or "I forgive myself and all others relative to whatever took place, or whatever role any of us played in it, for even if I my mind can't make sense of it now, I know I will understand it better someday, or upon my return to nonphysical". Know these truths, believe then, and this will assist in releasing the tethers of the vibrational impact of this topic within you.

10. Prayers of gratitude and/or expressing thoughts of love and appreciation are wonderful, powerful blessings that provide energetic support in your journey to wellbeing.

    Pray daily if you would like, perhaps each morning as you awaken, each night before you go to bed, even more often if you prefer, making each prayer a statement of love, care, and/or appreciation for anything or anyone that you feel gratitude or appreciation for, or for the presence of something or someone you desire already being in your life..

If you're feeling a bit off, in a valley, or having a rough moment, pray a prayer of appreciation for, memories of some of the most beautiful, perhaps even awesome experiences in your life, someone you especially love or treasure, or anything at all that you truly feel appreciation for.

Whether these or a prayer of silence as you perceive the flow of the beautiful air within you, or the nourishment it provides to your body, express joy, love, or wonder toward anything or anyone here or who has returned to nonphysical, of the joy and love and light that you shared or that you look forward to continuing to share throughout eternity, all such prayers will be in perfect, and be in absolute alignment with the health and wellbeing you are creating.

In those times when you feel on top of the world, you know who you are, and what you are creating, prayers of gratitude for your beautiful body, for the health and wellbeing of your body, and for all the fun and awesomeness that awaits you in the next 50 or other number of years of your life that you choose, the vibrations you emit through the feelings and emotions you experience while doing so will be filled with value, worth, perhaps even inspiration, each of which is are all the more helpful to the return to health and wellbeing of your human energy body that you desire.

Should you prefer to pray to Jesus, to any other individual aspect of the creator, or to the creator, statements of appreciation for your life, for their presence and support in your healing journey, for the infinite love they have for you, exactly as you are throughout the entirety of your life, and feel free to tell them how much you love and appreciate them too, and how you look forward to the ever more peace, joy, love, light, and fun that awaits you both upon your return to nonphysical,

Thank every single person who is in any way involved in your return to health journey, from your family members to your friends, any and all the varying medical professionals or alternative practitioners and/or resources you may be choosing to assist you, take the time to thank yourself each night before you go to sleep for the healing you created that day, and/or thank yourself when you awake in the morning for giving yourself the gift of life this brand new day.

11. Imagine yourself doing things you love to do with huge, specific detail. Literally envision yourself having those experiences, as granular as can be. Smell the air of the ocean you're visiting, of the flowers on the pathway or garden you're walking through, or of the pine trees in the majestic mountains or valleys you're exploring. Envision whoever it is you desire sharing these journeys or experiences with you, making them feel as lifelike as possible.

Perhaps focus on the "bucket list" experiences you've identified throughout your life, being on the trip or trips in the locations you desire, envision yourself laughing and having fun.

Imagine yourself driving the bright shiny convertible you desire on a beautiful sunny day, standing in awe as the garden you always wanted is now flourishing, playing with your children or grandchildren, walking on the beach, taking the sailboat or hot air balloon ride, sipping incredible wines in the Napa Valley or in Italy, enjoying the almost 24/7 fun and activities on the cruise ship, or even looking back over your life at 90-some years of age filled with overflowing gratitude and appreciation for all the life you've lived, all the joy and love you've experienced, the healing you experienced so many years ago, and equal gratitude for the incredible health you've experienced ever since, and your crystal clear awareness that each and every such person you have come to know or love will be sharing eternity with you as each of your respective life journeys become complete.

12. Begin a practice of sitting quietly, ideally in a place of peace or quiet you favor, perhaps even outside, close your eyes, and begin to sense your breathing;

As thoughts begin to arise within your awareness, simply let them pass, and return to your focus on your breathing.

Begin by doing so for a few minutes, perhaps once or twice a day, such as when you awake, before you go to bed, or if there is a common time that could work for you most days.

The more we exist without thought, the more peaceful it becomes within us, inside of us.

Engaging in this practice even once or twice each day helps us to connect with our higher selves, our eternal presence that exists within us throughout the entirety of our earthly journey.

This process creates space within us, it allows us to simply be, rather than always doing, which helps us become ever more adept at connecting with and/or otherwise perceiving subtle perspectives the universe seeks to share with us.

This process also gives us respite from the mind chatter relative to matters that are important to us, such as our health, progressively replacing vibrations we may be emitting that are not in alignment with our desires, replacing them with states of peace and calmness that are very much in alignment with our desires.

The more we practice this process, the more we are able to access and/or engage it in most any time or situation that arises within our lives.

Each of these practices, or any others that lead you to feel the emotions of joy, peace, love, freedom, wellbeing, value, worth, enthusiasm, appreciation, or any positive emotions represent wonderful tools that are available to you throughout every moment of your healing journey and will profoundly positively impact the manifestation of the healing you desire.

The final source of influence we will address relative to healing through this process is the choices we make relative to the specific processes, procedures, methodologies, and individuals and/or groupings of people that we choose to lead, engage in, or otherwise assist us in our healing journey.

The numbers of choices available in each of these categories can range from multiple to seemingly endless, some of which are in alignment with others, some represent varying degrees of contrast to others.

Achieving and believing in what you perceive as the optimal choices of people and practices to lead you to the healing you desire is an essential key to achieving the health and wellbeing you desire through this process.

It is equally as possible for multiple people experiencing similar health imbalances within their energy bodies to achieve healing through the engaging of differing people, practices, and/or methodologies they believe in due to the correlation of the influence of our beliefs on the outcomes we experience.

Should you seek assistance from any others in this process, it is important to select people and/or processes that you feel within you are capable of guiding and/or assisting you in your journey to create the healing you desire.

As you talk with the varying people, sense, and feel the feelings and emotions that arise from the thoughts they are sharing, and/or the practices they are defining.

Take time throughout the steps of this process to reflect within, fully understanding your eternal, limitless value and worth, that there are many paths that will assist you in releasing and/or healing from this temporary imbalance within your energy body, and as you feel the feeling of being healed within you, you will likely also begin to perceive which of the pathways you are considering feel in greatest alignment within you.

Given your likely heightened awareness relative to the energy nature of your body, you may also want to consider whether the opportunities you identify feel to be in alignment with, or contrast to, the wellbeing of the energetic nature of your body.

Will this process or procedure provide greater support and assistance to your energy body, or does it feel like it will place ever greater strain on your energy body that is already experiencing imbalance?

It is equally possible to achieve the successful outcome desired by not engaging other people or practices with others in your healing journey.

The first manner in which you could do so would be to identify and/or establish specific practices in your life to assist in the restoration and wellbeing of your energy body.

Ideas such as meditating, eating only healthy, natural, non-chemical, hormone, or antibiotic processed foods, taking peaceful walks or hikes once or more each day, spending time each day focusing on people and/or experiences that cause greatest feelings and emotions of love, care, and wellbeing to swell within you, or reading books or watching movies daily that bring these same feelings of joy, love, light, peace, and/or wellbeing.

The second manner in which one could achieve the successful outcome desired without the engagement of other people and/or practices similarly represents the second, separate process through which the desired can occur.

Jesus spoke the words "Blessed are those who believe who have not yet seen.".

These words of truth reflect the potential power of our belief.

While it is essential for us to believe in whatever people and/ or processes we choose to incorporate in our healing journeys is the first process of healing we define, it is equally possible for us to achieve this same outcome by truly believing within us that it will come to be.

A brief reflection upon these words leads to the clarity that he was speaking of the creation process through these words.

Said another way, should the undeniable, crystal clarity one holds within them, and, therefore, vibrates into the universe, be of the health and wellbeing of their body, this consistent, steadfast vibration could not help but result in the restoration of health and wellbeing within such person.

Yet it is important to state that, while emitting this vibration alone would certainly be sufficient for it to come to be, the simultaneous or even periodic emitting of vibrations doubting or questioning this process or their return to health could make it more challenging, if not difficult to experience the outcome we desire, depending on the strength (feelings and emotions) and frequency in which such doubting or conflicting vibrations are emitted.

The universe understands what we desire in the moment we perceive it, regardless of the circumstances that brought such desire to us and is eternally dedicated to bringing our desires to us.

Would we have no resistance, so to speak, or thoughts or vibrations in conflict with our desires, they would all come to be, just as they naturally do in nonphysical.

Yet among the greatest gifts of physicality is the ability to eternally choose what we focus on, to which the universe innately, naturally, immediately begins to respond and draw ever more to us in alignment with our vibrations.

Relative to healing, once our desire is determined, it is up to us to get into vibrational alignment with our health and wellbeing, regardless of how we choose to do so, and it will be; it is only us, or our minds, actually, that potentially stand in the way of us receiving what we desire.

And so, it behooves each person who seeks to achieve and/ or restore health and wellbeing of their energy body to determine the manners and resources they believe and that feels in greatest alignment within them to assist them in their healing journey, and as they continue to maintain this vibration throughout the entirety of their healing process, the natural, inevitable outcome will be the healing they desire.

It is a profound blessing to know that the ability to heal rests within us regardless of whatever health imbalance may come to exist within us until such time as the eternal aspect of ourselves, the very same aspect that chose for us to live this life experience, chooses for our life journey to be complete.

The entirety of the awareness we have shared brings us to the identification of Eternal Truth Number Five:

> *The ability to heal from any health imbalance exists within us throughout the entirety of our earthly journey; we accomplish healing by discerning and engaging in whatever resources and/or manners that feel in alignment within us, believing we will experience healing through such choices, and maintaining our energetic alignment with the health and wellbeing of our energy bodies throughout whatever pathway to healing we select.*

CHAPTER 6

Why Have We Come Forth, The Purpose of Life

Early on we established the truth that the vast primary, if not the sole element of our physical bodies is energy.

We then clarified the truth that this energy that exists within our physical energy bodies is the same energy that exists within every single element of physicality throughout physical existence.

We then defined this energy as the spirit of infinite intelligence and unconditional love of the creator, for it empowers and enables every single element of itself to exist, to make whatever choices it desires within each life experience in physical form that it chooses, and because it loves, cherishes, and treasures each and every individual aspect of itself throughout the entirety of each and every such temporal life experiences it chooses, and the entirety of its eternal existence.

So why would individual aspects of this spirit, this conscious-ness, these extensions of the creator of all that is choose to experience life experiences as human beings on earth?

For the fun of it.

For the joy of it.

In full, absolute awareness of, and unbridled enthusiasm for knowing each new life that each chooses and lives in human form presents their eternal being with ever new contrast, that such con-trast causes new desires to arise within them, that they will focus on their desires to attract them to them in their lives, all of which naturally results in growth and expansion of the respective individ-ual soul experiencing it, all the souls who in most any way interact with it throughout its life experience, and the oneness of the creator within which all exist throughout eternity.

Each such new life experience represents a brand-new oppor-tunity to "play in the sandbox of eternity", so to speak, in ever new ways throughout eternity.

Each and every time any individual aspect chooses another life experience in physical form the consciousness within them grows and expands.

It expands when they experience love, it expands when they experience hate, it expands when its current life experience becomes complete at 100 years of age, just as it expands when its current life experience becomes complete within hours or days of when it was born, or perhaps even before it is born.

There are no common end goals, or check lists of expectations, so to speak, which are expected of those who choose to live life expe-rience as human beings, other than for each and every such soul to experience and create in manners unlike any have before, or will ever come to experience again, each of which are natural results of the eternally unique contrast each experiences throughout the entirety of the life experiences they experience in physical form.

It is through this masterful methodology of weaving through and within each and every such life experience each chooses that the awareness and experiences of each such individual aspect of the divine grow ever more exponentially throughout eternity.

Each and every such life experience lived contributes exponentially to the eternal growth and expansion of the soul experiencing such experiences, and the oneness of the consciousness of the creator within which all exists.

There is so very much more to life than has generally been passed down, or that most have begun to understand.

The eternal essence of all that is - is love.

The eternal essence of all that is - is joy.

The eternal essence of all that is - is radiance.

The eternal essence of all that is - is peace and playfulness.

The eternal essence of all that is - is expansion of the consciousness of the oneness by each and every aspect of the oneness growing and expanding through each and every life experience each chooses throughout eternity.

We choose to come forth to live life. We choose to come forth to experience ever new contrast, ever new life circumstances, in the full awareness that we create from such experiences based upon what we focus on, and as there are limitless choices for us to focus on in physicality, the opportunities for us to grow and expand are equally limitless.

As the consciousness within us grows and expands with each and every such life experience, the state of full awareness of all that is within which we existed prior to our current lives necessarily becomes left behind, or temporarily suspended, so to speak, when we enter our physical lives to enable us to experience life experiences within our lives that differ from those we experience when we are in the state of full awareness.

The life experiences we experience in physical form differ greatly from those in nonphysical, just as they do from one another in human form, all the more so as we become aware of who we truly are, of the limitless ability that exists within us to create and live as we desire and choose to consciously create in ever new manners throughout the remainder of our current earthly journey.

It is for this purpose this book has been written.

As all are individual aspects of the divine, all are divine.

All are of infinite value and worth, all are worthy of all they desire, just as they are welcome to choose to create as they desire, and each such life experience each chooses brings ever greater joy, love, light, and awareness to the soul who experiences it.

While all such life experiences bring eternal growth and expansion to our souls, those who become aware of the truths of who they are and of the innate ability to create within them become empowered to experience ever more that they desire throughout their life while they are living them, rather than waiting until they return to nonphysical to experience the joy and love and light they desire again.

All come forth knowing full well that any current life experiences we perceive as joyful, loving, peaceful, or light filled become powerful catalysts for us to create ever more such experiences in our lives, just as life experiences we perceive as negative or hurtful are powerful catalysts to choose and create ever more of the opposite of these in our lives based upon what we have now experienced.

While sprinklings of human beings such as Jesus, Buddha, Einstein, and others have shared teachings of and lived their lives in manners in which others observed them creating as they desired within their life experiences, such teachings have not become common knowledge to most as of the time in which this book is being written.

It is now up to each who has become aware of this ability to choose to perceive it as their truth, and to consciously choose to live and create as they desire from this point forward in their lives, just as each is similarly welcome to not perceive this ability as their truth, or to allow their lives to continue to unfold in whatever alternative manners they choose.

Regardless of the choice or choices each makes, each and every we live is of profound benefit to the eternal growth and expansion of the eternal aspect of who we are individually, as well as the oneness within which all exist collectively.

This is the purpose and truth of each and every life experience choose, including and especially this one.

Live, explore, run, jump, sit, roll over, read 1 or 10,000 books, leap from the highest cliffs, fall in love with yourself and with others, hike in the Himalayas, snorkel or dive in the Great Barrier Reef, sing in an opera in downtown London, walk in the vastness of the Saharan desert, live in the midst of the most populus cities of the world, or in a cabin on a remote stream or mountain, have no children, or 27 of them, ride your favorite bicycle, drive your favorite car, become a rocket scientist, or the person who sweeps the floors at the end of each school day.

Ponder what brings you joy and happiness, and whatever else you desire in your life, and begin to perceive the action steps that present themselves to you to assist yourself in experiencing ever more of these in your life.

The process of feeling the feelings of what you want to be doing

or experiencing is the equivalent of planting, watering, and nourishing the seeds for such desires to come to be in your life; knowing
they will come to be is the sunshine that brings all such experiences
and even more into our lives.

Don't worry, be happy is a song that millions throughout the
world are aware of, while also the recipe for bringing all we desire
into the lives we came forth to live.

It truly is that simple.

Together the entirety of these insights weave into Eternal Truth
Number Six:

> *We are eternal aspects of the creator who
> have chosen to come forth to live our eternally
> unique, current life experience. The purpose of
> our life is to experience ever new contrast and
> engage the innate ability within us to create
> all the more we desire throughout each such life
> journey we experience.*

CHAPTER 7

Our Minds

Our minds can be among the greatest blessings of our lives.

They are profoundly powerful, far beyond that of the most advanced computers that exist today or will ever come to be.

They have the ability to perceive vast, virtually limitless thoughts, ideas, and perspectives, to ponder and contrast differing concepts, to calculate, to strategize, to figure out the simplest or most complicated dilemmas or challenges, to develop and integrate varying levels of knowledge and awareness relative to virtually limitless different topics throughout our lives, to communicate, and so very much more; the memory storage within them is virtually limitless throughout the progressive tenure of our lifetimes.

Beyond these varying ranges of capabilities that assist us in navigating and processing within our daily lives, an additional, key aspect of their primary function is to protect us from harm.

As an example, if we place our hand on a hot burner on the stove, the awareness of the pain we experience will lead our minds to develop a default perspective of heightened awareness within them that will present itself as we find ourselves in similar situations or environments where such occurrences could potentially cause us harm again throughout the rest of our lives.

A second primary manner in which our minds function is their ability to classify and/or categorize the virtually limitless forms of contrast and occurrences we experience throughout our lives.

From early on, we are exposed to perspectives shared with us from others, such as parents, relatives, caregivers, schoolteachers, or others we are exposed to that tell us or have experiences with us, which our minds accept as truths, generally without questioning when we are young.

Simple examples include someone telling us we are smart or so especially cute/attractive, or perhaps dumb or ugly; others may tell us other people, such as those of differing political perspectives, or of different colored skin, are good or bad, or right or wrong/

As we grow older, especially throughout our teems, our minds begin to develop and engage filters in which they determine or perceive themselves whether perspectives or other communications that are being shared with, taught, or told to us by other people or sources to be truthful.

The result of such filtering activities, or the varying degrees they apply such filtering to can also become selective based upon the source of such perspectives.

Automatic acceptance may be the choice for all such perspectives an individual or grouping of people they trust or admire shares with them, just as automatic non-acceptance may similarly occur relative to individuals or groupings of people they do not trust, or who they determine to be a source they do not feel in alignment with.

Examples of such "default" filtering could be that of automatic acceptance of perspectives individual or groupings of their peers present to them during their teenage years, and automatic rejection of perspectives their parents share with them during this same segment of their lives.

Alternatively, our minds tend to also identify people and/or groupings of people throughout our lives in which they will, by default, accept, either temporarily or permanently, all the perspectives and/or teachings of specific people and/or groupings of people in our lives.

Examples of this could include individual and/or collective groupings of friends that we interact with directly, or others, such as people we become exposed to through media or who are presented to us by our friends who we seek to emulate.

Our minds may also become progressively more open to sensing what they perceive as truths over time, even of those they previously perceived as those they chose not to accept such perspectives from, perhaps focusing on the data or information itself, rather than the person or groupings of people sharing such information.

Parents could be a good example of such progression, the perspectives of which were previously discarded due to their perception of the source, then later accepted based upon the perspectives or other information they share.

Alternatively, some similarly become progressively less open to perceiving perspectives from others, possibly any or all others, perhaps holding tight to, or even being gripped by perspectives their minds hold tightly within them, or memories of past experiences of hurt or pain in their life, by not feeling connected, or not feeling love, or of not perceiving themselves to be of value or worth.

Such individuals may avoid and/or pull back from interactions and/or experiences with select other individuals or groupings of others their minds have somehow categorized as bad, wrong, potentially hurtful, or simply of no value to them.

And so our minds continually gather and process information throughout our lives, including and especially through the varying life experiences we become exposed to, accepting varieties of perspectives as its truths, others as untrue, the totality of which becomes the kaleidoscope through which they view and perceive our lives and the world and happenings within it around us..

Armed with these perspectives and our mind's default intent to protect us from what it perceives as potential harm to us, our minds projects perspectives to us in alignment with the totality of the filtered perspectives of truths it perceives.

One such example would be that which we shared previously, of making sure we keep our distance from, and/or are especially careful when we are near or using a stove to keep us from burning ourselves again.

Our minds presenting such perspectives with and/or directions to us are certainly logical and will serve us well throughout the longevity of our life experience.

Yet there are similarly situations in which our mind's process of analyzing layering, and/or categorizing the information, circumstances, and experiences we've had throughout our lives leads it to present or project perspectives to us may not be in alignment with the truth of what a new opportunity, experience, person, or grouping of people are presenting to us.

As an example, perhaps a person had a relationship in which

they cared for the other greatly, and while the person cared for them in a similar manner for a time, a time came in which they no longer cared for them in that manner, and the person experienced hurt.

The hurt could have been so great that the person's mind could lead them to do all it can to keep them from any such future experiences in which such hurt could take place, or automatically push them away from further opportunities they somehow came to experience in which they began to feel the same feelings with others that resulted in the hurt or pain that followed with one or more people in their past..

While this may appear to be a logical perspective for a mind to consider, it is equally logical to consider that, with all the people in the world today, certainly there are viable candidates who similarly seek to share the exact same lifelong relationship of joy, love, and partnership that we desire with us that would not result in the same outcome as that or those they previously experienced.

The perspectives our minds present to us in some situations, or relative to certain specific topics in our life, can be in contrast to what we truly desire, and what is truly best for us, yet due to their ever expanding ability to expand the intensity of the perspectives they share with us, left unchecked, the resulting fear we experience can keep us from engaging in any such potential relationships with others, or from staying in a relationship with the most perfect person who seeks the exact same that we do, and with whom the result would be very different from that which was experienced in the past..

On a related note, imagine a person in our lives who is critical of us – potentially consistently throughout the entirety of our life.

You are not as attractive as others, or perhaps even ugly, you are dumb or stupid, or not capable of doing many things, or perhaps most anything right, how could you do that, why didn't you do that, how can you not be as good as others, look at how you embarrass yourself, why aren't you as successful as others, or look at how you fail in all the relationships you experience; can't you do anything right?

While the list of such criticisms could go on and on, the last thing we would want in our lives would be to have any other person in them who communicates with us in such manners; and yet the minds of almost all people communicate with them in this manner at least occasionally in their life, some in this manner more frequently, the minds of some communicate with them in this manner consistently, if not ever more progressively throughout the entirety of their life.

Such circumstances represent a critical distinction for those who experience them that is essential to address for those seeking to consciously create and achieve all they desire in their lives.

Just as we are not our bodies, neither are we our minds.

Yes, our minds are a part of who we are, they are profoundly capable in so many differing ways, and they can be exceptionally helpful to us, blissfully so in many aspects of our lives, or in certain periods of our lives.

Alternatively, they can also be among the most critical, judgmental, disempowering, and hurtful components of our lives; a times, perhaps even cripplingly so.

So why would they do this to us? If they have the capacity to perceive and do so many things we define as good, why would they present perspectives, at times, or depending on the topics, unrelentingly, that figuratively or literally cause us harm, or keep us from experiencing that which we choose, perhaps even long to experience in our lives?

A helpful manner for us to address this essential topic is to create a perspective in which we view our minds as computers.

Computers have the ability to do amazing things; our minds have the ability to do even more.

And yet, as computers function based upon the programs entered into them, our minds function in a generally similar manner as well.

As an example, let's say that we were having fun with a group of friends when we were young, and someone walks up to us totally out of the blue and says "Do you have any idea how ugly you are?" in front of them all.

To make things worse, one or more of our friends with us – perhaps even our closest friend or friends – followed that person when he or she walked away from us, stopped being our friend, or no longer associated with us after that occurrence had taken place.

While there is certainly no truth relative to such a comment for any human being, and the catalysts for the person making such a comment may have been jealousy because they perceive us as attractive, or more attractive than they perceive themselves to be, because we have a group of nice friends they don't have, or because someone such as a parent, sibling, or friend said or did something equally as hurtful to them, and they are looking for some relief from how bad they feel, from such an experience could easily become the equivalent of planting a seed, or installing a program into our minds that we truly are what we were told.

It is not uncommon for our minds to present such perspectives to us as we move through our lives, perhaps even flooding us with such perspectives that became planted within us that are consistent with the criticism, fault, blame, or shortcomings others somehow communicated to us throughout our lives, or to project such past perspectives on our current life experiences.

Even without such external experiences, in ages such as our early teens when we see others on TV, in movies, or perhaps even musicians or others we become exposed to via social media that we find attractive or admire, such observations could easily perspectives within our minds of us not being attractive, of value, or of worth.

As we become aware of the truths that we are all eternally unique individual aspects of the divine, of limitless value and worth exactly as we are, throughout eternity, and that we are all blessings of beauty, joy, love, and light throughout the entirety of our eternal existence, the awareness of these absolute, eternal truths alone could progressively assist us in releasing such perspectives to the contrary our minds present to us, and/or assist us in progressively re-programming our minds in a manner that reflects these truths relative to who we are.

We have also previously identified a practice that is capable of assisting us in receiving, enjoying, and experiencing the gifts and blessings of the mind, while no longer be subjected to the hurtful, disparaging, or limiting perspectives it presents to us.

As stated before, when we feel good, or any of the range of feelings in that generic category, the perspectives we are choosing are in alignment with our souls, the eternal aspect of who we are.

We also clarified that, when we feel bad, a lack of value or worth. or any feelings or emotions in the range of these, it is not because of what we have experienced, or witnessed taking place around us, it is because the perspectives we are choosing in that moment are not in alignment with our souls, the eternal aspect of who we are.

Our awareness of these differing states empowers us to accept the perspectives our minds present to us that make us feel in the generic range of good, kind, loving, or caring as our truths, and to not accept such perspectives our minds present to us that feel in the generic range of bad, judgmental of ourselves or others, of a lack of value or worth as our truth.

As we now know the truths relative to who we are, we become empowered to select and/or bask in the perspectives we choose to be our truths, and release those we do not choose as our truths without in any way negatively influencing our lives.

This simple practice is profoundly effective in assisting us in releasing undesired perspectives that have previously come to exist within us; our choice to focus ever more greatly on those that feel in alignment naturally bring ever greater joy, love, light, peace, happiness, and all the more we desire into our lives.

Should such "negative" perspectives feel difficult to release or should one's mind be bombarding them with multiple such perspectives, two powerful, effective ways to shift the nature and/or frequency of such experiences include creating space when they arise within us, and shifting our focus to anything we feel gratitude or appreciation for.

The concept of creating space when such occurrences take place can be as simple as taking a deep breath or two, standing up, walking away, or any physical movement or mental shift in which we no longer "go down the rabbit hole" of allowing our minds to further expand upon the perspectives it is attempting to present to us.

Taking a deep breath or two and/or focusing on such deep breaths as we are taking them for a couple or more minutes is a wonderful way to create space in such situations; those who become aware of the truth of who they are will find equal results by sharing a statement such as "I am of infinite value and worth, exactly as I am." in that moment, the result of which will similarly, immediately create the shift we desire when we truly sense and perceive this truth within us.

Relative to our ability to shift our focus to anything that brings us feelings of gratitude or appreciation in such moments, there truly is no limit in the number of topics we can focus on to expand the emotions of gratitude or appreciation within us.

Whether the feeling of appreciation for the air that you breathe, the sunshine outside, the feeling of the wind or gentle rain on my face, or the thought of your partner, child, the fun of a recent experience you had, a memory of joyful, loving, or light-filled experience you had recently, or perhaps long ago in your life, the pondering of your favorite meal, or taking a walk in the park, any and all such experiences will ideally, wonderfully, and perfectly replace any perspectives to the contrary that our minds present to us in the moment, while progressively lessening the frequency of the presentation of such perspectives to us over time.

Our minds are beautiful gifts, they are profound blessings, and essential elements of our physical life experiences.

Depending on the programming we were exposed to prior to developing filters within us, or subsequent "truths" they adopted later in our lives based upon experiences we experienced and/or witnessed others experiencing, and our previous lack of awareness that perspectives they present to us are not who we are, rather choices for us to consider, this awareness is the key that progressively releases such perspectives our minds previously held, and unlocks the potential for us to experience ever more of all that we desire within our lives.

This precious and beautiful outcome is available to those who consciously choose to develop such new relationships with their minds, for the result of the practice of releasing perspectives that do not feel good within us and replacing them with those that feel good naturally results in a corresponding shift of the vibrations within us, which naturally engages the universe to bring ever more to us that feels in alignment within us.

Harmony in our relationships with our minds, the result of being aware the perspectives our minds share with us are but perspectives for us to consider, is among the greatest gifts we can give to ourselves.

The ability to achieve this precious, beautiful state exists within all, and will assuredly lead all who consciously choose to engage with their minds in this manner to a life filled with ever greater joy and love and light than you have ever known before, while releasing themselves from further harm, hurt, or pain their minds previously caused them to experience.

The totality of this discussion relative to our minds leads us to Eternal Truth Number Seven:

> *Our minds are limitless blessings. The perspectives they present to us are choices for us to consider; those who choose to discern the perspectives they share, release those that do not feel in alignment, and focus ever more greatly on those that do feel in alignment are forming a pathway to ever greater peace, joy, happiness, love, light, and all we desire coming to be in our lives.*

CHAPTER 8

Our Hearts

Relative to the physical functioning of our bodies, our hearts represent the organ with primary responsibility for the functioning of our human energy bodies; they also represent the primary source of the energy of our lives.

Our hearts also represent our direct connection to our souls, the eternal consciousness who has chosen to come forth to live the life experience in human form that we are living.

As discussed previously, when we feel good, or any of the range of feelings and/or emotions that in any way support, uplift, or empower us, or bring ever greater joy or love or light into our lives, it is because we are perceiving ourselves, our current circumstances, life experiences, and/or the action steps we are taking in alignment with this eternal, unconditionally loving aspect of who we truly are.

Alternatively, when we feel bad, or any of the range of feelings and/or emotions that in any way criticize or lead us to feel guilt, shame, judgment, unworthiness, anger, malice, distain, disappointment, or revenge relative to ourselves or others, individually or collectively, it is because the perception we are choosing relative to ourselves, our current circumstances, life experiences, and/or the action steps we are taking in contrast with this eternal, unconditionally loving aspect of who we truly are.

The emotions and/or feelings we perceive as we navigate our way through our life are perceived within our hearts.

These indicators reflect whether we are in alignment with those of our souls in every given moment of our lives, or out of alignment with those of our souls in any given moment of our lives.

Our souls eternally hold crystal clarity relative to the radiance and perfection of who we are, and know no judging, perceptions of wrongdoing, blame, fault, or any such perspectives that are negative in any way relative to who we are, who any and all others are, or the manners in which we or others live our lives.

Our souls are aware that such perspectives represent those of our minds, and in no way reflect any truth relative to who we or others are.

Our souls always perceive us with love, and as love.

Our souls perceive all others with love, and as love as well.

The love, care, appreciation, admiration, and cherishing they hold for us and all others never ceases, rather it continually increases throughout eternity.

Our souls are never separate from us, nor can we ever be from them, for they are the eternal essence of who we are.

Similarly, our souls are all individual aspects of, aka extensions of the divine, and as we are our souls, we are similarly individual aspects of, aka extensions of the divine

As the physical universe innately brings ever more to the individual aspects within it that is in alignment with the vibrations they emit into it, how divinely blessed human beings are to have the innate indicators of feelings and emotions within us that continually reflect whether the perspectives we are choosing in any given moment throughout our lives are in harmony with those of our souls, or in contrast to them.

Such indicators are not in any way attempting to tell us we are right or wrong in a given moment, or good or bad in any way, rather they serve as guideposts, so to speak, to reflect to us whether the thoughts, words, beliefs, and/or action steps we are taking in any given moment are in alignment with those of the eternal aspect of who we are.

What difference does it make if our choices in any given moment are or are not in alignment with those of our souls?

There are two primary answers to this question.

The first is that we know what we know based upon what we have learned and/or experienced to this point in our lives, and what we see around us.

The scope of awareness of our souls represents the totality of all that is, not the temporal subset of such that allows us to have our current life experience in physical form.

In simplicity, the perspectives of our soul are rooted in vastly expanded awareness beyond that of our minds in our human experiences.

The second answer to this question is that our soul is us, it is who we truly are, and for this reason, it seeks for us to have and to experience all that we desire in our lives, without limitation.

For this reason, and combined with its broader awareness, it knows and sees pathways to all we desire, and is eternally dedicated to assisting us in experiencing all we desire throughout our temporal human journeys.

As a result, the greater the alignment with our souls that we choose to life and experience, the greater the peace, joy, love, light, and manifestation of all we desire that we experience in our lives.

So… what does this eternal aspect of who we are want from us?

It wants us to live, to love, to explore, to move about the world of physicality around us, to experience ever new experiences, ever new contrast each and every new day, and from such contrast create ever new desires, experience our new desires, and from such new vantage points as these desires become manifest in our lives, create ever new desires, and "play in the sandbox of life" in whatever new ways that we feel inspired to experience within us.

There is no checklist, no common pathway, no default process that is any more right than others, or wrong way to live our lives, so to speak, for as we have stated before, each and every life experience we experience throughout eternity exponentially contributes to our growth and expansion throughout eternity.

Experiences in physical magnificently differ from those in non-physical due to the differing circumstances and contrast each innate within them, all of which differ from those of others such lifetimes, or what others experience within the same lifetime, for as change is constant throughout eternity, each and every life experience each has throughout eternity will be unlike they or any others have ever experienced before or will ever experience again.

It is for this reason that physical existence came into being; to allow the creator, through all the individual aspects of itself, to experience and create in ever new ways throughout the entirety of the varying life experiences they choose to experience throughout eternity.

And so, a partnership of sorts awaits us all with our higher selves.

We can live, love, sashay, and knock around, so to speak, in whatever manners we wish; choosing to do so in alignment with our souls, which are never separate from us, and always experiencing all that we experience with us, holds the potential for a continuity and progression of ever greater joy and love and light and manifestation of our desires beyond that which most consistently experience in their lives.

The key to perceiving our alignment with our souls rests in the internal indicators of the feelings and/or emotions we perceive within our hearts.

Severn years ago, I woke up in the midst of a two-week vacation visiting a friend in a small Costa Rica village on the Pacific Ocean sensing a feeling to go within me.

My mind knew I was in a breathtakingly beautiful small village spending time with my friend each day, swimming and snorkeling on its award-winning beach, fully recharging charging the batteries of my life, enjoying amazing space, time, food, and more.

Yet, as I had come to trust the feelings inside of me building up to that moment in my life, I gathered information as to the country to the south, the north, and felt alignment within me to head to Nicaragua in the north, in spite of the fact I had never been to that country, aspired to go there, or known anyone who had ever been there.

I then selected my mode of transportation, perceived a city I would travel to, found a hotel that felt in alignment on a park in the middle of the city, and headed north.

Four nights later I had a "movie-like" experience meeting a woman as I walked in the restaurant that I felt the nudge to eat in that night.

I had been divorced for 16 years, the feelings I felt as I met her represented the totality of those I defined throughout the years since, continuing to follow what felt in alignment within has resulted in the most precious sharing of life together with her ever since.

Our hearts are priceless sources of the internal indicators of feelings and emotions within us; our souls have crystal clear awareness of our desires, and limitless awareness of how to bring them to us.

Should we choose to sense, feel, or otherwise perceive the messages they share through our hearts within us ever more progressively throughout our lives, we will experience ever greater joy, love, light, peace, preciousness, radiance, and manifestation of our desires throughout the entirety of our lives.

Together these insights and perspectives lead us to Eternal Truth Number Eight:

> *Our hearts are the primary source of life for our energy bodies, and the internal source through which we perceive feelings and emotions, which serve as internal indicators of whether the thoughts or beliefs we are holding within us, words we are speaking, or action steps we are taking are in alignment with the perspectives of our souls in any given moment throughout our lives.*

CHAPTER 9

Death

The perspectives previously addressed within this book together weave a foundation of awareness within which the truth relative to the concept human beings refer to as "death" can be easily perceived and understood.

In simple essence, the experience human beings refer to as death is an experience in which the soul, the eternal aspect of each individual, withdraws itself from the temporal vessel of their human body, and returns to full re-immersion in nonphysical, the state of existence and full awareness in which it existed prior to its current earthly journey.

The process of the soul's return to nonphysical separating itself from its life experience in human form is as natural and expected part of its human life experience as its birth is at the beginning of their human life experience.

Like the choice each soul makes from its state of eternal awareness to enter a new life experience, each soul similarly chooses from this same state of eternal awareness when its current life experience is complete.

As the soul is eternal, and all are respective aspects or extensions of the oneness within which all exist, the return to nonphysical is the experience all souls experience as their respective life journeys become complete.

Our souls are also aware that all relationships are eternal, and as all return to nonphysical when their current life journeys are complete, any and all souls can choose to maintain, expand upon, and/or experience ever new interactions and relationships in ever new ways as each desire individually, or any numbers of such desire collectively, throughout eternity.

Souls never experience reservations or fear relative to their return to nonphysical; to the contrary, as their awareness of the perfection of the timing of their transition, and the limitless and ever-expanding opportunities that await them to experience as they desire throughout eternity becomes fully reestablished upon their return to nonphysical, they are simply aware of their transition to be a perfect, natural, fundamental aspect of their eternal existence.

This awareness remains complete until such time as each soul chooses to enter into another life experience in physical form, should they desire to do so, at which time their awareness shifts to that of the form of life they choose to experience, which is most commonly another life experience in human form once they have lived one or more life experiences in human form.

Alternatively, each soul is similarly welcome to continually exist in nonphysical throughout eternity, should they desire to do so, or to mix and match life experiences between physical and nonphysical as they desire throughout eternity.

Upon each soul's return to their state of full consciousness in nonphysical, all are welcomed home, so to speak, and experience overflowing joy, love, gratitude, appreciation, and enthusiasm for its precious radiance and existence, for the entirety of the experiences it experienced in its physical experience, for all who in any way shared the briefest interactions or longest life experiences with them, and for its return to the expanded awareness that it and the creator, the oneness within which all exists, has now experienced based upon the entirety of the life experience it experienced..

These truths are as absolute as they are universal; they apply equally to each and every person who has ever lived, who exists today, or who will ever come to be.

Like the atoms within our earthly bodies, all souls are individual elements of the whole, of limitless value and worth, exactly as they are, equally contributing to the eternal expansion of their respective souls, and the oneness within which all exists, throughout eternity.

While large percentages of humanity have been introduced to, and/or come to believe and/or fear that their transition will be followed by some sort of analysis, judgment, or ascertainment as to whether certain beliefs or practices have or have not been achieved in their life, action steps have or have not taken, or whether the lives they lived have fallen short of any necessary or essential elements or requirements in some way, no such truth exists relative to any such perspectives.

In truth, such perspectives are in direct contrast to the fundamental nature of eternity, of the oneness within which all exist, and the eternal perfection of all, exactly as they are, throughout the entirety of eternity.

Similarly, while many perceive the value and/or worth of certain individuals or groupings of people to be greater or less than others, and/or that the destination that awaits them when their life journey ends somehow differs from that which other individuals and/or groupings of people will experience, no such truth exists relative to such perspectives.

As challenging as it may be for human minds who have somehow come to perceive through whatever source or sources have led to such perspectives existing within their minds, the truths defined throughout the entirety of this book have identified the simple, absolute, unequivocal truths that apply equally to all who have ever been, all who exist today, and to all who will ever come into being, that:

- All are individual aspects within the oneness of the divinity of all that is,
- All are of limitless value and worth, exactly as they are, throughout eternity,
- Each and every life experience in physical form creates growth and expansion of the respective individual extension of the whole, while simultaneously of the oneness within which all exist,
- The creator, the source that enables and empowers the existence of all that exists, eternally loves, cherishes, and treasures each and every individual aspect of itself, exactly as all are, throughout eternity,
- The creator is equally present within every single one of the individual aspects of itself throughout the limitless life choices each makes, whether in physical form or nonphysical, throughout eternity.

- That the process of the reciprocity of consciousness in which the individual extensions of the source of all life and of the source of all life itself together grow and expand through each such life experience each individual aspect chooses throughout eternity represents the manner in which all together experience growth and expansion throughout eternity.

These truths epitomize the unconditional love of the creator, the source of all life, the endless and ever-expanding love, care, and appreciation of every single aspect of itself that ever comes to be, and each and every millisecond of their existence throughout whatever forms of life each choose to experience throughout eternity.

As such, there are no conditions upon which one could be separate from the creator, disappoint or displease this eternal consciousness in any way, or somehow be judged or otherwise be perceived as bad, wrong, or falling short of any expectations by the creator or any others for anything they did or did not say, do, practice, or live in their lives.

The creator is also equally aware of the limitless value of contrast in the life experiences each of the extensions or itself choose throughout eternity, the richness of which represent the primary reason for physical existence to come into being, for it is the limitless forms or variations of contrast that naturally lead to limitless new creations by the individual aspects of the source of life who choose to experience life experiences in physical form..

While the minds of human beings have evolved in manners in which many perceive varying forms of contrast as good or bad, or right or wrong, neither the creator nor our souls perceive such perceptions.

Instead, whatever has taken place simply is, and from this new viewpoint, awareness, or perception that has arisen based upon what has taken place each is now welcome to create anew.

More accurate descriptors of all that takes place in physical existence represent the state of the individual aspect or aspects creating them to be either in alignment with their souls, and, therefore, the source within which all exist, or not in alignment with these eternal aspects within us all.

Once any and all such occurrences and/or experiences are created, the response of each who witness or otherwise become aware of such creations may similarly be in alignment with our souls, and, therefore, the oneness within which all exist, or not in alignment with these eternal aspects within us all.

While many choose to focus on why or how occurrences and/or experiences have come to be, the rightness or wrongness of such experiences, or who to blame for experiences that created outcomes not desired by others, those who choose to experience ever greater alignment within and draw all the more they desire to come to them in their lives are better served to find alignment within, aka with their souls in such circumstances, and to shift their focus to what they now desire in light of what has taken place.

As all souls are eternal, all relationships are equally eternal, therefore the ability to interact with fellow souls throughout eternity allows us to have ever more physical experiences with one another as each desire throughout eternity.

In this same spirit, as all return to the state of consciousness and full awareness of all that is the moment their life journey in physical form becomes complete, each similarly achieves crystal clarity relative to the contribution every single experience, occurrence, exchange, or interaction we experienced individually or with others throughout our lives was to our life journey.

In this awareness, we not only love, cherish, treasure, and experience profound appreciation for the individuals and interactions that brought varying levels of joy, love, and/or light into our lives, we similarly experience equal love, cherishing, treasuring, and profound appreciation for the individuals and interactions that brought what we experienced as difficulties, pain or hurt in our lives.

As eternal beings, each of us has experienced exceptionally wide ranges of experiences throughout the entirety of our existence to this moment in eternity.

It is the experiencing of both ends, aka positive and negative, so to speak, of experiences that lead us to ever greater expansion throughout eternity. We have similarly brought and/or shared experiences of both ends to others throughout the entirety of the life journeys we've shared.

The incredible amazingness of what a life filled with love can be is all the more incredibly experienced when one has experienced a life they perceived to be void of love.

The richness of a life experience in which we assist one or others who have limitations of any sort become infinitely greater when we live a life in which we experience such limitations.

It is this eternal process that leads to ever greater growth and expansion of all throughout eternity.

As we approach the conclusion of this chapter, it may be helpful to share some additional perspectives relative to souls returning to nonphysical, or whatever subsequent life experiences each choose to experience in physical form throughout eternity.

Each such life experience in physical form that each chooses is eternally unique, the awareness within each life experience is eternally unique, and the vessel of each new human energy body is similarly eternally unique.

We do not come back to relive our prior life experiences; we come forth to live ever new, once in eternity life experiences in new energy bodies that are optimally aligned with the new life experiences we are experiencing.

While the awareness of all we have experienced throughout eternity and of all that is continually exists within our souls throughout eternity, we naturally enter each new life experience as a "blank slate', so to speak, upon which we can draw and create anew as we desire throughout the entirety of our new life experience.

It is not uncommon for us to experience new life experiences with fellow souls we've danced with in the past, perhaps even many times, or perhaps new souls we choose to dance with that we have not shared lives with in physical form in the past.

This is not to say that our lives are predetermined, as each is truly living and creating their lives anew each new moment of each such life experience they choose, yet multiple souls of any number may choose to share experiences with others individually or collectively.

A concept of karma has come to exist that will be helpful to briefly discuss as well.

Certainly, we have identified and addressed the creation process in exceptional detail, and for this reason, it is truthful to state that we draw to us ever more that is in alignment with the vibrations we emit into the universe throughout the entirety of each and every life experience we choose to experience throughout eternity.

Thus said, it is important to clarify that no truth exists within the inherent perspectives of karma being a retribution of some sort based upon wrongdoings we have caused to other individuals or groupings of people, or such fault or blame being carried from one lifetime to another to "pay us back" for perceived harm what was caused.

No one beyond the human mind is taking score or categorizing things or behaviors or experiences as good or bad, or right or wrong, and, therefore, prescribing some such compensating experiences in our current or any other future life experiences we choose to experience.

Instead, each lives each new moment of each and every new life experience they choose capable of creating what they desire within such life experiences based upon the vibrations the emit into the universe.

While no such thing as karma exists, the fundamental similarity the concept of karma has relative to the creation process is that, unless the vibrations each emit in the future differ from those they emitted in the past, the experiences of the individual in such life experiences will remain largely similar throughout their entirety of their lifetime.

The process of creation separates from the perspective of karma in this important regard, however, for should the individual who is likely unconsciously creating their life in manners they do not desire shift or otherwise modify the vibrations they emit to those they now desire in light of all that has taken place to any point in their life, the life experiences the individual experiences will similarly shift to become in ever greater alignment with the new vibrations such individual is emitting into the universe.

It is also helpful to clarify that each soul is responsible for their respective life journey throughout the entirety of their life journey.

All souls came forth in full awareness of this truth, all know they are loved so much that they are welcome to choose whatever life experiences they desire throughout eternity, just as they are welcome to create as they desire within each such life experience.

They are also equally aware that all other souls have similarly come forth to live their lives as they desire, create as they desire within their lives, that each soul is on their own respective life path, and that no others have come forth to in any way correct, fix, or take responsibility of the life path or paths of others.

While we may choose to assist other individual or fellow groupings of souls in varying ways, no souls have come forth with the intent to impose their wills, perspectives, or beliefs on others, rather to establish and live our lives in awareness with what feels in alignment within our own soul, while similarly walking and/or otherwise interacting with others who cross our paths who are similarly living their lives in manners that feel in alignment within their souls.

It certainly is helpful and in alignment to provide for the basic needs of children when they are young, yet as our souls are equally aware they came forth to live their own lives, helping them experience the greatest freedom possible while loving them for who they are, exactly as they are, assist them in developing their internal awareness of alignment within them, and, therefore, creating whatever feels in greatest alignment within them in their life.

It is for this same reason that progressively greater conflict often arises in the raising of children due to their desire to teach them what is right and wrong, and/or to control the lives of their children.

A child who knows, senses, and perceives they are loved regardless of the decisions they make will live a very different life path than one who consistently feels a lack of love due to the control a parent and/or other adult attempts and/or succeeds in exerting on them.

As the exact children are born to the exact parents at the exact time, among the greatest gifts we can give to others, regardless of the circumstances of how they have come into our lives, including our children, is to be in our own alignment, which naturally leads to us recognizing the infinite value, worth, radiance, and perfection of who all others are, exactly as they are.

This is the equivalent of our soul recognizing theirs, in full awareness their earthly journey is as perfect for them as ours is for us, that we have both come forth to create as we desire within our lives, and that the exact life journey they are living is the most divinely perfect life experience for their soul, just as ours is for our soul.

The final aspect we will address that is directly or indirectly related to death is that there is no accident, so to speak, relative to the conditions within which the soul withdraws from the human energy body, nor is the soul ever harmed in any way in this process.

Like the perfection of the parents each soul experiences their life through, and the timing in which their human life begins, the timing it chooses and manner in which it separates from its human body are equally perfect from the perspective of the soul, regardless of whether such manner is perceived to be logical or harmful to their human mind, or the minds of others.

As each is eternally interwoven with all others, the timing and circumstances within which each transition are as similarly perfect for each who was in any way connected to them in their lives, though some, if not many may not perceive the clarity of how this could be until their return to nonphysical.

Thus said, the truths identified within this book are capable of assisting those who perceive themselves to be "left behind" to understand the transition of loved ones and/or those held in highest regard represents new contrast for them to create upon, and the awareness the love they shared has neither ended or lessened in any way, rather became ever more enriched as any conditions or limitations to this love they may have previously perceived within their minds no longer exist.

The process of transition is truly a time of celebration for all, including the one who transitioned.

While it may be natural to grieve for the individual and the changes in life that occur to those remaining in their human bodies for a time, celebrating the life of the one who transitioned, continuing to sense, perceive, receive, and share love with this soul may be helpful to consider, while the greatest gifts we can give to them, and to ourselves, is to continue to live our lives in ever greater peace, joy, love, light, and harmony with our desires until such time as our souls choose for our life journeys to become complete.

These writings lead us to Eternal Truth Number 9:

> *Death is the natural process in which our soul withdraws itself from the temporal human energy body it experienced it's physical life experience through and returns to the nonphysical state of full consciousness and awareness at such time as it determines it has experienced the fullness and perfection of its current human experience.*

CHAPTER 10
Expanding Our Consciousness

There are limitless manners in which we can experience ever-expanding consciousness throughout the entirety of our earthly journey.

The truth of this statement rests in the awareness that there are limitless, ever new manners in which we can experience ourselves and our lives in light of the continued expansion of our awareness of the truths we have identified within this book, and of the integration of them into our lives.

This truth applies to each and every human being individually; it equally applies to each and every grouping of two or more human beings collectively.

Awareness is the essence of consciousness. It is not a destination, rather a journey each and every individual aspect of the creator is experiencing in their own eternally unique ways throughout eternity.

It is a state of being that influences the manners in which we live our lives.

Every time we experience life in new ways our consciousness expands, our vibrations expand, and we are simultaneously then presented with ever new viewpoints from which to experience our lives.

From these new viewpoints we perceive new desires, we birth them into being by our focus on them, and the universe then dedicates itself to bringing our new desires to us.

This continual process throughout eternity is the purpose for which we chose to come forth to experience our current human journeys, just as it was for all life experiences we have ever lived to this point in eternity and will be for each and every life experience we will experience throughout eternity from this point forward.

And so the intent of this final chapter is dedicated to identifying manners capable of assisting individual aspects, and/or groupings of such aspects, in weaving ever expanded consciousness into their pathways throughout the remainder of their current earthly journey.

Certainly, each and every experience we experience has the ability to expand our consciousness, and for this reason, we will address this topic by defining eight categories of manners in which we can achieve this goal within our current lifetimes.

In no certain order, they include.

How we perceive and interact with ourselves:

The individual aspect of the creator that we know the best, that we spend the entirety of our life with, that we experience the entirety of our earthly journey with, and that most profoundly influences who we are, the manners in which we live in our lives, and the manners in which we create in our lives, whether consciously or unconsciously, is ourselves.

We have clarified how all are individual aspects of the divine, that all are of infinite value and worth, exactly as they are, and that each is living a life that is as perfect for their soul as ours is for our soul.

These same truths apply to each of us as well, and knowing and living these truths with ourselves is among the greatest gifts we can ever give to ourselves or to others.

It is among the greatest gifts we can give to ourselves because it continually forms and influences the manners in which our lives unfold.

Should we understand that we are individual aspects of the divine, we will understand that we are similarly of infinite value and worth, regardless of how our lives have unfolded to this moment in eternity, or how they will continue to unfold throughout the remainder of our earthly journey.

We will understand that we deserve whatever it is we desire, and as we learn to progressively shift our focus to be the presence of whatever we desire already being in our lives, ever more that we desire will naturally flow to us due to the vibrations we will be naturally emitting in our lives.

We will be ever nicer to ourselves, all the more so as we become ever more adept at progressively releasing perspectives our minds present to us to the contrary, and replace such perspectives with words, feelings, and emotions, of how beautiful, loving, kind, caring, and especially capable we are, exactly as we are.

Engaging in ever more respect, care, and appreciation of who we are, words of praise, and kind actions toward ourselves similarly continually expands the vibrations we emit into the universe to be more positive, loving, and caring, to which the universe will naturally respond by bringing ever more in alignment with these fundamental energetic attributes that we vibrate into it to us.

Truly loving, caring for, and appreciating ourselves in ever greater ways similarly ever more greatly expands our ability to live our lives in similar manners to others too, for as we no longer seek to find blame, fault, or wrongdoing in ourselves or others, we become ever more capable of living in manners of alignment with ourselves and others.

The foundation of our relationship with others do not rest in the others, rather within ourselves.

Should we be in alignment, perceiving ourselves to be of value and worth, we are able to recognize, honor, and engage with others in manners of alignment.

Should we not be in alignment within ourselves, we will not be able to establish true alignment with others, for the kaleidoscope through which we perceive others will be influenced by the lack of alignment within us, and not allow us to fully recognize, honor, and engage with others in manners of alignment.

The opportunity to perceive, love, cherish, care for, and truly appreciate ourselves is among the greatest ways for us to experience ever expanding consciousness, and to be fully capable of experiencing expanded consciousness in limitless other ways throughout our lives as well.

How we perceive and interact with others:

Just as the choice to recognize and celebrate the preciousness and amazingness of who we are naturally shifts the unfolding of our life experiences forevermore, so also do these same practices as we engage these same practices relative to all others.

Previously our minds largely dictated the manner or manners in which we perceived others, and our default acceptance of such perspectives as truths naturally influenced the manners in which we interacted with such individuals or collective groupings of people.

As we are now aware of the eternal beauty and perfection of who all others are, exactly as they are, of the entirety of their life journey being as perfect for them as ours is for us, no longer will we succumb to such perspectives of lack or limitation of our love and care for others, exactly as they are; instead, we will progressively experience ever more joy, love, caring, light, and appreciation for all others, exactly as they are.

How ever more refreshing life becomes as we become progressively more adept at truly perceiving the beauty and majesty of all others, exactly as they are.

Regardless of the color, the words they speak, the beliefs or practices they hold within their life, the manners in which do whatever they do in their life, or the perspectives they choose relative to religion, politics, or any and all other potential topics that exist, simply witnessing and appreciating them for who they are, the life they are living, and the blessings they and their lives are to us all results in us experiencing ever greater joy, love, and light in our lives, as well as share similar energetic vibrations of love, light, worthiness, and appreciation to all other individuals and/or groupings of people that we choose to perceive and/or interact with in such manners.

A tremendous burden is lifted from us as we become progressively ever more adept at releasing perspectives of blame, fault, wrongdoing, or jealousy, and forever replaced as we choose to perceive others with ever greater peace, joy, love, light, and acceptance of all others, exactly as they are.

Do you want to see the face of God?

Then look into the face of any and all others that exist, for each is an individual aspect of, an extension of, an equally essential, integral component of the creator incarnate.

Look in the mirror, for this person who is seeing the face of God in all others is a face and being of the source of all life too.

It is in all such interactions that we have with any and all who cross our paths in any way that we are engaging, interacting, and/or otherwise experiencing life in ever new ways with the creator itself.

Loving, respecting, and cherishing of all others we choose to be in relationship with, that we interact with in the briefest moments of our lives, the seemingly most minimal manners, or perhaps throughout the entirety of our lives, for each such occurrence, each such relationship, is a precious and beautiful way for us to experience ever greater consciousness within us in such interactions, with any and all such fellow individual aspects of the divine, and with the entirety of the consciousness within which all exists.

Our relationship with the creator, with consciousness, with the source of all life:

The varying aspects and references we have identified relative to the creator allow those open to perceiving alignment with these truths to release perspectives they have somehow come to perceive that are not in alignment with these truths.

As we release such perspectives of as a human being-like figure, for such aspects exist only in physicality, that this eternal consciousness as somehow watching over us to someday account for mistakes or disappointment it perceives based upon manners in which we lived or did not live our lives, we are, in the process, expanding our consciousness relative to the creator, and paving a pathway for an ever more beautiful relationship with this source of eternal life for all.

Understanding this consciousness as the eternal source of unconditional love that it is, and that we and all others are extensions of this eternal preciousness, represents the epitome of consciousness; choosing to live our daily lives in this awareness results in ever new manners to experience ever expanding consciousness within us, and also throughout the entirety of interactions we have with others.

As all others are aspects of this oneness within all that exists, each and every interaction we have with others represents an interaction with the source of all life, and holds within it the innate gift of ever expanding awareness.

As delightful and radiant as such experiences can be, experiences of equal, if not greater contrast to these equally empower such individual aspects who experience or witness such experiences to experience ever greater consciousness in light of whatever it is they witness or experience.

Consciousness is a presence, it is a state, it always exists, while is similarly influenced by all that takes place.

The innate source of all consciousness is that of unconditional love.

All experiences that take place result in the expansion of this consciousness of unconditional love, and no such occurrences or experiences can exist outside of unconditional love, for unconditional love is the innate, eternal state of consciousness.

Yet we ourselves can connect with ever more of it, aka expand our alignment in ever greater alignment with it, all of which expands our consciousness, all of which represents ever expanded alignment with the creator, and expansion of the consciousness of this eternal source of all life.

It is simply not possible to do wrong, for all that takes place leads to ever expanding consciousness, though the ability for us to experience ever greater consciousness in our varying lifetimes through our awareness of the creator and ever greater alignment with all who cross our paths in our daily lives is among the richest, most beautiful, and precious ways to expand our consciousness with the creator.

As we complete our discussion relative to this topic, a song comes to mind that I taught to groupings of children in vacation bible school years ago.

The words "Laugh, shout, dance, and sing, and have yourself a ball, we were meant to share, our lives with one and all, love, one another, and your brothers, and siters too, we need each other, we need each other, our whole lives through" are moving within me as the words of this topic are flowing through me.

In essence and simplicity, these words represent a wonderful roadmap to expanding our relationship with the creator and our consciousness, for in such actions, perspectives, and experiences, we are not only viewing the lives we are living, and those of others in manners that are in complete harmony with the joy, love, and light of the creator; this eternal source of all life is similarly experiencing all such experiences with us.

And so the potential for us to experience our relationship with the creator through others exists in ever expanding ways.

Talk with the creator. Thank this consciousness of all that is for all that is. Express gratitude or appreciation for any and all aspects of life, or occurrences that take place.

See and talk with God in the sunrise or the moon at night, in the deepest moment of love and connection you feel, in the birth of a child, the transition of a loved one, in the new bright, shiny thing you once desired and have now received, in your favorite meal or treat to eat, talk opening with this spirit on your way to or from work, or attend any form of gathering in which people are expressing gratitude or appreciation for whatever the topic may be.

Each of these are wonderful ways to expand our relationship and consciousness with God throughout our lives.

Witness and marvel in the growth arising from the newly planted seed, the children playing in a playground, pets or animals in their respective majesty, the trees swaying in the breeze, the incredible uniqueness and radiance of each flower, the forms of physicality that support our earthly journeys, such as the homes we live in, the clothing we wear, the food that we eat.

Among my most favorite ways to connect with and experience the creator are when I choose to be in silence.

Years ago I found this state to be somewhat difficult to achieve, I have since learned to experience it most any moment I desire, and in this space I feel such a profound, deep gratitude and appreciation for all, I feel such a closeness to God, and I truly feel one with all that is.

There is no wrong relative to communicating with the creator, for in true essence, we are literally doing so throughout every moment of each life journey we choose to experience throughout eternity, all of which naturally expands our consciousness through each and every such moment we experience.

How we choose to live our daily lives:

While the opportunity to expand our consciousness is always available to us, people, events, and experiences, aka varying forms of contrast, continually present themselves to us throughout our earthly journeys that can make it seem challenging, if not impossible to achieve such expansion within our daily lives.

The greater truth is that the manners in which we perceive, experience, and move through all such forms and/or sources of contrast represent among the greatest manners in which we can expand our consciousness throughout the entirety of each and every life experience we experience throughout eternity.

Years ago, I watched a movie I perceived to be a waste of my time, and one I had no interest in ever seeing again.

Perhaps a decade later I perceived an interest to watch it again, and when it did, it quickly became among my favorite movies due to the very different perspective in which I perceived the movie.

Entitled "Groundhog Day", the essence of the movie I perceived in my second and many subsequent viewings of the movie is that, while the world around the main character was the same as he muddled through each consecutively repeating day of his life experience early on in the movie, the experiences he experienced in it began to change as he changed who he was and how he interacted with others in each new repeating day version of his life experience

The end result as multiple such repeating days of his life had unfolded was vastly different than those in which the movie began, both for the main character himself, and also for virtually all of the people he interacted with each day, regardless of the degree or apparent significance of their interactions.

We are the creators of our daily life experiences through the vibrations we emit throughout the entirety of them, while the universe is continually bringing ever more to us in alignment with what we emit into them.

One who daily focuses on ever greater lack or things not working for them most every new day will be rewarded with ever more experiences of lack, and things not working for them as their life and their repeated perspectives continually progress.

One who begins to find anything to focus on that brings them feelings of peace, joy, love, happiness, or appreciation most every new day, perhaps even including people and/or circumstances they previously perceived as frustrating, angering, or disappointing to them, will be rewarded with ever more experiences of peace, joy, love, happiness, and appreciation as their life and their repeated perspectives continually progress.

Regardless of how we have lived our lives to this point, each and every new day represents a new opportunity to determine who we choose to be, how we choose to interact with ourselves, and with all others in the world.

The ability to continually expand our consciousness exists through all we experience depending on how we choose to perceive the contrast we experience.

Our consciousness eternally expands with the more joy, love, fun, or appreciation we express or experience in our lives, for each of these will come back to us in ever new ways as we choose to live our lives in this manner.

Conversely, experiences that bring the opposite of these to us, such as anger, disappointment, feelings of guilt, or unworthiness, represent important decisions for us to consider.

Should we become wrapped up in them, perceive ourselves as helpless victims of whatever has taken place, continually tell stories of them to others, or blame or find fault in ourselves and/or others for what has taken place, it is difficult for our consciousness to expand in such moments due to the manners in which we are perceiving what has taken place.

Alternatively, such experiences similarly represent powerful opportunities to expand our consciousness, for as the purpose of contrast is to create ever new desires, those who choose to focus on the new desires that arise from such experiences will find them to be wonderful, if not profound ways for us to expand our consciousness, while simultaneously bringing ever greater joy and love and light into our lives.

The reference to the process of expanding our consciousness is truly nothing more than the byproduct of living and experiencing life anew each day.

Yes, our consciousness does expand at least somewhat in the worst of our days, yet celebrating all that brings good feelings and/ or emotions to us, while shifting our focus from all that brings bad feelings or emotions to us to most anything that does feel good, or what we now desire based upon such contrast that has been presented to us results in far greater expansion of our consciousness, as well as a life filled with ever more of all we desire coming to be in our lives.

There is no end goal, or form of measurement, so to speak, relative to the expansion of consciousness within our lives; nor is it possible to somehow assess or otherwise measure the "quantity" of consciousness each is achieving.

Neither is there a race, or competition to somehow achieve more than others, for among the greatest awareness's of consciousness is that each is experiencing their respective, perfect life journey, equally expanding their consciousness in ever new ways throughout eternity.

The entirety of the life experiences we choose to experience throughout eternity naturally and innately expand the consciousness of our soul through the ever-new life experiences they experience within each such life each experience.

Said another way, all continually expand our respective individual consciousness throughout the entirety of all that we experience throughout eternity.

While the degree to which experience expanded consciousness within each such life journey may vary based upon the alignment, and/or lack thereof, we experience within each lifetime, the expansion of the consciousness of our souls is equally perfect as each such life journey becomes complete and will continue to expand ever further through each and every subsequent life journey they choose to experience throughout eternity.

The release of the need or desire to control others:

Whether individually or collectively, none have come forth with the intention to control others, nor with the intent to be controlled by others.

Freedom is a key, eternal essence of life for all throughout eternity.

Freedom allows us to be who we choose to be, to experience what we choose to experience, to perceive what we experience in whatever ways we choose, to create whatever we desire within our lives, and to live our lives in whatever manners we desire.

As all have the ability to focus as they desire, all have the innate freedom to create as they desire in their lives, regardless of the circumstances they are experiencing in their lives.

Just as the creator creates, all that is created creates, all of which expands creation and contributes to the ever-expanding consciousness throughout eternity.

While all are welcome to create as they desire, the essence of seeking to control others rests in perceptions of lack or unworthiness.

Varying percentages of human beings seek to control others to gain more for themselves, or for their minds to somehow perceive them of being of greater value or worth through their control of others.

Those who become aware of the truths within this book will no longer seek to control others., for they will engage the creation process to create whatever it is they desire, while ever more clearly perceiving their infinite value and worth exactly as they are.

As ever more are progressively shifting their perspectives from seeking to control others to seeking to empower others, the expansion of consciousness taking place within humanity is becoming unprecedented.

As change outside of us always begins with change within us, choosing a shift from control to empowerment within ourselves and of all others in our own lives ever further expands the shift taking place within humanity from that of control to that of empowerment.

And so how perfect it is that some seek control, while others become controlled, for as each experiences either aspect of control, whether the one who controls or the one being controlled, the perspectives they choose resulting from such circumstances they experience assists each in creating new desires within them, and manifesting such new desires in their lives.

At the same time, how freeing it becomes to those who initially sought to utilize control of others to make themselves feel of value or worth, or to achieve greater earthly resources within their lives, to realize they already are of infinite value and worth, exactly as they are, and that the ability to achieve whatever earthly wealth they desire innately exists within them, regardless of whatever circumstances they may currently be experiencing in their lives.

From pushing against to creating anew:

From an energetic standpoint, pushing against anything naturally perpetuates and/or further expands that which we no longer desire to experience.

Neither aggression, conflict or war create peace or joy; peace, joy, love, and light create peace, joy, love, and light.

As ever more become aware that this simple truth applies equally to all individually, and the entirety of humanity collectively, practices of conflict, or seeking to cause harm to ourselves or others in any way, are soon becoming mere chapters in history books, and will no longer exist within humanity.

As pushing against anything represents our continued energetic focus in alignment with what we no longer choose to experience. advocating for, aka focusing on what we instead desire brings ever more in alignment with our desired outcomes to us.

This truth differs from perspectives many have held throughout the evolution of humanity, and many still perceive today, for varying forms of contrast have existed in manners which have been perceived by the minds of some or many as bad or wrong, and as such, it was equally logical to such minds to attempt to fight against., if not eliminate whomever or whatever was somehow involved in whatever it was they no longer sought to experience.

The awareness we have now achieved empowers us to perceive and respond to such forms of contrast in manners that will truly lessen and progressively eliminate perspectives of fighting against and/or eliminating others by instead shifting our focus to what we now desire.

Like worry, pushing against anything or anyone further expands the numbers of people and/or experiences for us to push against, while focusing on, envisioning, and believing what we desire will come to be naturally results in bringing ever more of what we desire to us.

Those who seek peace will no longer focus on war, those who seek wellbeing will no longer focus on imbalance, those who choose love will no longer focus on hate, those who seek abundance will no longer focus on lack.

Individually or collectively, as ever more progressively shift their focus from what they are pushing against to that which is now desired, the expansion of ever greater joy and love and light humanity experiences as a result is as vastly limitless as it is unprecedented.

Experiencing greater consciousness in relationships with others:

Understanding the endless, eternal value and worth of each person provides a wonderful foundation from which we are able to achieve greater consciousness in our lives through

relationships with other fellow aspects of the divine.

Our awareness's that it is the uniqueness of each and the differences in the manners in which all experience their lives that leads to the eternal growth and expansion of all enables us to release perspectives of disappointment, judgement, anger, or jealousy of others we may hold within us and empowers us to shift our perspective to that of appreciation of each living their lives exactly as they are.

This new foundation of awareness expands our ability to achieve greater consciousness in relationship with others.

Understanding that each is responsible for themselves is an additional truth that expands our ability to achieve greater consciousness in relationship with others, for this perspective recognizes the same ability within and freedom of others to live their lives in whatever ways they desire that exists within us as well.

And so, our ability to experience expanded consciousness in relationship with spouses, life partners, family members, or others we choose to have closer relationships with eternally rests within us.

That is not to say that all relationships will be built upon foundations of mutual love, caring, or admiration, for this would require both to perceive or desire this same outcome from the relationship they experience with others.

Instead, consciousness in relationships represents us perceiving and holding all others in a place of care, respect, appreciation, and awareness of their perfection exactly as they are regardless of the manner in which they perceive or hold us within their awareness.

Those who seek to dance or otherwise play in the sandbox of life in any way with us represent opportunities for us to expand our consciousness by being ever more aware of the radiance and perfection of each such individual, and appreciation for who they are, exactly as they are.

Those who do not choose to dance or play in the sandbox of life with us, or with whom we have had experiences that did not result in peace, joy, happiness, or mutuality of respect, care, or wellbeing similarly represent opportunities for us to expand our consciousness by being ever more aware of the radiance and perfection of each such individual, and appreciation for who they are, exactly as they are.

The reminder that all relationships are eternal is helpful to reintroduce here, for while we may or may not understand why others feel or behave a certain way relative to us, we know all is well either way, that there will be a time in which we will be able to understand how such feelings or behavior have come to be, such as upon our return to nonphysical, and that it does neither we nor them any good for us to create or hold any stories within us as to why others feel or behave in such ways.

In our awareness that focusing on what does not feel in alignment within us naturally draws ever more that does not feel in alignment to us, it will serve those who seek to exist in ever greater alignment to consider following some guidance Jesus shared in this regard with his disciples relative to such relationships we experience in our lives.

He spoke of "Shaking the dust off your feet" by simply walking away and moving on in your alignment while allowing the other to do as they desire from such interactions as a helpful perspective that allows each to move on as they desire, and to experience expanded consciousness through such relationships.

Certainly, his consciousness was far beyond that of forming opinions of such individuals or groupings of people as bad, wrong, of less value than him or others, making up or telling of why they were wrong to somehow justify he was right, or causing harm or some form of retribution to any they had such experiences with.

Instead, this simple wisdom he shared allowed him and those who followed him to continue to recognize the divinity and perfection of all regardless of their interactions with him.

There is an additional, key aspect that is important to clarify relative to expanding consciousness, as well as ever greater joy, love, and light within relationships.

Among the greatest contributors to relationships not working rests in the perspectives our minds present to us in such relationships.

Our awareness of and ability to discern and release perspectives that do not feel in alignment with the relationship we desire together empower us to create and experience relationships we desire within our lives.

Peace, joy, happiness, and love are among the greatest blessings we can experience in relationships with others.

Using the example of partner relationships, they generally initially form and expand based upon seeing, sensing, and/or otherwise experiencing a form of attraction of these or other such perspectives in others.

As time passes, it becomes common for minds of human beings in relationships to shift their focus to undesired aspects of that person, things they say or do, or the way they live their lives.

It may be cute or playful to witness them tossing their clothing in a pile on the floor as they join us in bed the first nights they spend with us, yet at time passes, perspectives of disappointment, if not anger may arise within our minds following such occurrences due to the mess of the clothing they never seem to want to pick up to help us keep the room clean.

The minds of many in relationships progressively shift their focus to presenting an ever-growing list of things that result in disappointment or anger within us as the tenure of our relationship continues to unfold.

Such perspectives may even progressively fester within us, potentially even boiling over at times, either of which lead to a lessening of the joy or life or light we experience in such relationships, at best, if not a dramatic shift or change leading to the end of such relationships.

As we attract to us ever more of what we focus on, or hold within us, focusing on what our minds perceive as the faults or wrongdoing of others we are in relationship with naturally bring us the opposite of what most desire, and certainly the opposite of what we initially experienced in such relationships.

This same truth, however, can bring ever expanding joy, love, light, and appreciation to both in relationships in which they choose to release perspectives of such contrast their minds present to them, and continue to focus on the joy, love, and light they experience in the relationship, the beauty, preciousness, and radiance of the person they are choosing to share the relationship with, and memories of joyful and/or loving experiences they experienced in the past, or the envisioning of ever more such experiences in the future.

The same perspectives of creation relative to all the other aspects of our lives exist and equally apply within relationships as well.

Relationships of love and preciousness can continually grow and expand as each chooses to continue to focus on the love and preciousness they perceive within themselves, in those they choose to be in relationship with, and on the relationship itself.

Should either instead shift their focus to the perspectives their minds present that are not in alignment with a caring, respectful, and/or loving relationship, the progressive continuation of such focus cannot help but influence the experience each has in the relationship, perhaps to the point of ending the sharing of the relationship in whatever manner they had chosen, such as a marriage they shared together.

It is also helpful to clarify that the reason most minds present negative perspectives to those in relationships generally have nothing to do with the other person, rather the perspectives such as lack, unworthiness, jealousy, or failure in some manner such minds are holding relative to us in individual moments or experiences within our lives, or often progressively more commonly throughout our life.

Regardless of the cause for our minds presenting such perspectives to us, our awareness and willingness to sift and sort through the perspectives they present to us relative to the other person they are in relationship with represents the primary ongoing contributor to each having the ability to continue to experience the relationship each desire with the other.

While the forms of the relationships differ, whether they be with a single individual, or groupings of any numbers of others, opportunities for ever expanding richness, fullness, joy, and all we desire becomes ever more present within such relationships for those who choose to consciously engage in such practices relative to such relationships in their lives.

Experiencing expanded consciousness with our human energy bodies:

The simple essence of two different perspectives represents greatly expanded consciousness relative to our relationship with our human bodies.

The first is to treat our bodies with love, care, respect, and appreciation.

Talk with our body, thank our body daily for the blessing of our ability to live each day in it, and for each of the individual atoms coming forth to allow us to live as we desire and experience our life experience in human form.

Praising, thanking, and expressing appreciation to our bodies all represent vibrations of love and wellbeing.

Certainly, the gifts of our energy bodies represent all of these and more to us, and the additional, natural byproduct of such practices is the ever-greater expansion of all of these within us.

In addition to expanding ever more of the joy, love, light, and appreciation of our energy bodies in these or limitlessly other differing ways, we similarly experience ever expanding consciousness and blessings with our energy bodies by releasing perspectives of judgement of ourselves or others, hate, anger, distain, disregard, and other such crippling feelings and/or emotions from within them.

As the core essence of the energy that constitutes our energy bodies is unconditional love, choosing to, and/or to otherwise hold perspectives within our energy bodies that are not in alignment with these, perhaps even in great contrast with these, are literally toxic to our energy bodies.

Among the greatest contributors, and often the greatest contributor to severe illnesses and/or disease within human bodies, are the toxic feelings, emotions, and or memories we continue to hold within our human energy bodies, as such energies could not be in greater opposition to the unconditional love of who they truly are.

As an example, such contributors are among the two primary causes for cancer arising within people.

Holding extreme perspectives of hate, distain, or perhaps equally errant perspectives of ugliness or unworthiness of ourselves within human bodies whose virtual sole essence is unconditional love is toxic to our energy bodies; while they do their best to maintain wellbeing for as long as they can, the continued festering of such energetic imbalances within us eventually lead to health, aka energetic imbalances within our bodies.

This first primary cause of cancer is literally the energetic equivalent of our body's response to our holding of toxins, or poisons to our energetic bodies within us.

The second primary cause of cancer, as well as many other illnesses and diseases, is simply the result of the creation process being unintentionally applied and/or experienced by those close to and/or aware of such imbalances within others.

While likely none would ever consciously choose experience such an imbalance, those unaware of the absolute correlation between what they focus on and what becomes manifest in their lives, combined with this same lack of awareness in most others, can unintentionally lead to bring such illnesses or disease to their energy bodies.

Children or relatives of those who experienced cancer have higher rates of cancer occurrences because of their continued awareness of this energetic imbalance, the strong emotions they experience as those they love move through this process, and/or the expansion of fear within them relative to the possibility of them experiencing this same imbalance someday.

We are aware the continued progressive focus on any topic brings ever more in alignment with our focus to us, whether it is what we desire, or not.

Further, as the health care and pharmaceutical industries spend billions of dollars each year promoting the products and/or services they provide, the continued "dripping" of perspectives of illness, health imbalances, and progressive decay have become equally powerful contributors to the expansion of all such illnesses, diseases, and/or other forms of health imbalances within humanity.

The expansion of consciousness relative to our human energy bodies that awaits all in each new moment of our lives rests in our awareness of the importance of releasing perspectives of toxicity and/or poison from within us, and also include disengaging from forms of media focused on health imbalances, and remaining in alignment with our health and wellbeing within us, perhaps through a process as simple as thanking our bodies for our wonderful health and wellbeing as we begin and end each day.

Viewing such creative stimulus from an energetic standpoint, the essence of the outcome we desire is to "energetically unplug" such occurrences or perspectives within our lives from this point forward.

While "unplugging" or disengaging our focus from such media is as simple as avoiding such sources, disregarding any we somehow become exposed to, and replacing them with practices of appreciation of the wellbeing of our bodies, it may be of benefit to consider an additional process relative to the releasing of toxicities from within us.

In our awareness that it does not serve us to focus any further on the topic or topics that led to such powerful vibrations in contrast with wellbeing within us, the key to "unplugging" these memories and/or experiences rests in releasing such perspectives from within our minds.

In summary, clarity, and simple essence, it is the perceptions our minds continually hold relative to whatever has taken place that result in the presence and continuance of toxicity and/or poison within our energy bodies.

Depending on the severity of the experience or occurrence, it is certainly logical to hold strong feelings and/or emotions relative to whatever took place to cause the expansion of these within us, and the intent of addressing this topic is not in any way to say that what took place was deserved, that it should be swept under a rug, or that the person wanted such experience or occurrence, or were in any way to blame for whatever took place that led to the occurrence or experience they experienced.

Instead, the intent of the focus on this topic is to empower those who desire to release the emotions attached to such memories or occurrences, in the awareness this will progressively lessen and eliminate the energetic influence of such memories or experiences on our energy bodies.

Again, depending on the severity of the occurrence, this may not be easy, yet the awareness of our ability to release such perspectives from our minds, and the related energetic health imbalances from our life experience, together empower and enable those who desire to release such poisons from within their human energy bodies.

The process to do so basically rests in initially softening the perspectives of harm or wrongdoing being held within our minds and progressively replacing them with those in ever greater alignment with our health and wellbeing going forward.

In truth, had we not had that experience, we would not be the person we are today.

This statement may be as helpful to some, depending on what they experienced, as it is angering to others, for many human beings experience tragic life experiences.

This statement is not intended to somehow gloss over, or suggest people should just forget about such occurrences, as such outcomes are likely not even possible.

It is, however, intended to suggest that, regardless of what has taken place, and in full awareness that we are creating the new in our lives by what we choose to focus on in each new moment of them, those who seek to release the energetic influence of such poisons or toxicities from within their energy bodies will be best served to replace such vibrations with ever greater vibrations in alignment with health and wellbeing they desire.

As the primary key to our happiness and our pathway to the health and wellbeing of our human energy body rest in the vibrations we emit, developing and maintaining vibrations of love, light, peace, joy, and appreciation within us brings ever more in alignment with these into our experience.

These are truly among the greatest forms of consciousness we can bring and/or share with our human energy bodies.

As our human energy bodies are the vessels through which our souls experience their current earthly journeys, expanding our consciousness through ever greater alignment with the innate nature of peace, joy, love, and light within them is among the greatest gifts we can give to ourselves, and through which we and our energy bodies experience ever greater peace, joy, love, light, health, and wellbeing throughout the entirety of our lifetime.

Together these varying aspects relative to our consciousness lead to Eternal Truth Number Ten:

> *The consciousness of our soul expands through the entirety of the experiences it experiences throughout eternity; the ability for us to sense or perceive such expansion within our current life experience rests in our alignment with our souls, and the awareness, aka state of consciousness, within which we live and move through our lives.*

EPILOGUE

Jesus spoke and lived the words "You shall know the truth, and the truth shall set you free."

The ability eternally exists within us all to understand and live our lives in harmony with this truth.

He similarly spoke and lived the words "The kingdom of Heaven is within".

This is the awareness, the consciousness we experience as we live our lives in ever greater alignment with our souls.

As our souls are the eternal aspects of who we are, literally aspects, extensions, or expressions of the creator that eternally exist within the oneness of the source of all life, experiencing alignment within is truly experiencing alignment with the creator, aka the kingdom of heaven, within us, and within our lives.

The truths within this book are in alignment with these truths of which Jesus spoke.

The choices to perceive these truths as our own, or to live our lives in harmony with them, truly open us to the opportunity of perceiving ourselves as the creator does, all others as the source of all life does, and all that we experience within our lives and/or witness in others in alignment with the manners in which God does.

This opportunity exists within us each of us each and every new day throughout the remainder of our life journey.

Blessings, peace, joy, and infinite and ever-expanding love and light I wish to all, with equally infinite appreciation to you for being the exact, endlessly precious, radiant person that you are, and for following whatever pathway you perceived that led you to the truths we have defined within this book.

May even a single perspective within it, if not the entirety of all we have shared, will bring greater peace, joy, love, light, and alignment to you throughout the remainder of your earthly journey, and the eternity that awaits us all as our life journeys become complete,

Erik Swenson

March 28, 2023

CONTACT

Erik can be reached to coordinate seminars, workshops, presentations, public appearances, or weekend retreats throughout the world via:

www.10EternalTruths.com